STEP-BY-STEP

15-Minute
Vegetarian

Step-by-Step
15-Minute Vegetarian

Matthew Drennan

Photography by Amanda Heywood

LORENZ BOOKS

LONDON • NEW YORK • SYDNEY • BATH

To Mark and my parents, Jim and Betty, with thanks.

First published in 1996 by Lorenz Books

© 1996 Anness Publishing Limited

Lorenz Books is an imprint of
Anness Publishing Limited
Boundary Row Studios
1 Boundary Row
London SE1 8HP

ISBN 1 85967 174 8

A CIP catalogue record is available from the British Library

Publisher: Joanna Lorenz
Senior Cookery Editor: Linda Fraser
In-house Editor: Jillian Stewart
Designer: Alan Marshall
Photographer: Amanda Heywood
Home Economist: Stephen Wheeler
assisted by Lucy McKelvie

Printed and bound in Hong Kong

For all recipes, quantities are given in both metric and imperial
measures, and, where appropriate, measures are also given in standard
cups and spoons. Follow one set, but not a mixture, because they are
not interchangeable.

CONTENTS

INTRODUCTION

Vegetarian food has finally become a major part of our cuisine. We no longer need to justify the inclusion of vegetarian dishes on restaurant menus, and a cookery book such as this is to be universally celebrated and not seen as catering to the few. The notion that vegetarian dishes are uninspired, heavy and dull has long been dispelled, but one myth that does persist is the idea that vegetarian food is fussy and time-consuming. Fast food has become an important part of our culture. The demand for "real food" in this area is increasing, and vegetarian food is no exception.

Step-by-Step 15-Minute Vegetarian proves how easy it can be to produce a delicious vegetarian lunch or dinner in less time than it takes to reheat a ready-made meal from the supermarket. The emphasis is on freshly prepared produce cleverly coupled with staples from store cupboard or freezer.

The secret of success when speed is essential is to make sure you have all the ingredients and necessary equipment before you begin. Advice on stocking the store cupboard and what constitutes a survival kitchen is given on the next few pages. For quick cooking, cut ingredients to a similar size and remember that root vegetables will take longer than most greens. Master the "all hands on deck" method, using the time while one item is cooking to prepare the next, and you may be surprised to discover just how swift a cook you can be.

So whether you are a committed vegetarian, enjoy the occasional vegetarian meal, or just want something simple and satisfying because you are in a hurry or too tired to spend long in the kitchen, this book brings you the means of making fantastic home-cooked meals in moments.

The Store Cupboard

Your store cupboard should be the backbone of your kitchen. Stock it sensibly and you'll always have the wherewithal to make a tasty, satisfying meal. Begin with the basics and expand as you experiment, buying small quantities where possible and keeping an eye on "use by" dates.

OILS, SAUCES AND CANNED GOODS

Chilli oil
Use this fiery oil sparingly to liven up vegetable stir-fries and similar dishes.

Groundnut oil
This bland-tasting oil will not mask delicate flavours. It is good for deep-frying. Use vegetable or sunflower oil instead, if you prefer.

Olive oil
If you must have only one oil, a good olive oil will suit most purposes (except deep-frying). Extra virgin olive oil is more expensive and best kept for salads.

Sesame oil
Favoured in oriental cooking for its flavour, this rich oil can be used on its own or combined with vegetable oil.

Ghee
This is pure clarified butter. Used extensively in Indian cooking, it is usually sold in blocks or cans.

Black bean sauce
A thick aromatic sauce made from beans, used for marinades and stir-fries.

Passata
This thick sauce is made from sieved tomatoes. It is mainly used in Italian cookery.

Soy sauce
A thin, salty, black liquid made from fermented soya beans. Add a splash at the end of cooking and offer extra at the table.

Sun-dried tomatoes
These deliciously sweet tomatoes, baked in the sun and dried, are sold in bags or in jars, steeped in olive oil.

Tahini paste
Made from ground sesame seeds, this paste is used in Middle Eastern cookery.

Tomato purée
This is a concentrated tomato paste which is sold in cans, jars or tubes. A version made from sun-dried tomatoes is also now available.

Canned pulses
Chick-peas, cannellini beans, green lentils, haricot beans and red kidney beans survive the canning process well. Wash in cold running water and drain well before use.

Canned vegetables
Although fresh vegetables are best for most cooking, some canned products are very useful. Artichoke hearts have a mild sweet flavour and are great for adding to stir-fries, salads, risottos or pizzas. Pimientos are canned whole red peppers, seeded and peeled. Use them for stews and soups, but stick to fresh peppers for anything else as they lack the firmness of bite that is needed for dishes such as stir-fries. Canned tomatoes are an essential ingredient to have in the store cupboard. There is now a very wide range available, whole or chopped, plain or with herbs, spices or other flavourings. Additional useful items to include are ratatouille (make sure it is a good brand, though) and sweetcorn.

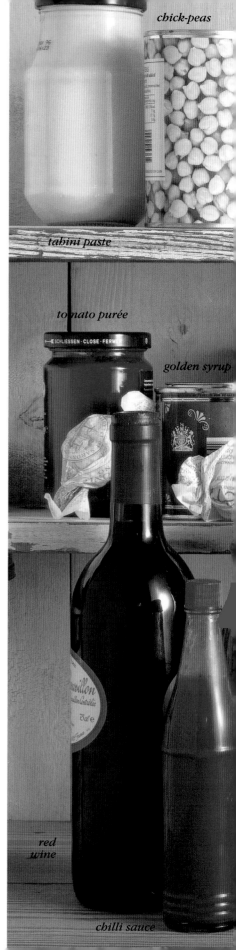

chick-peas

tahini paste

tomato purée

golden syrup

red wine

chilli sauce

chopped
tomatoes

chilli
oil

herb vinegar

pimientos

sweetcorn

black olive
paste

white wine
vinegar

ratatouille

kidney beans

lentils

chillies in oil

tahini
paste

soy sauce

plum tomatoes

olive
oil

black bean
sauce

mustard

honey

passata

groundnut
oil

red wine
vinegar

balsamic
vinegar

salad dressing

ghee

black olives

Dry Goods

Assuming your store cupboard already includes flours, sugars and dried fruits, the following items are invaluable for speedy cooking. The list of spices relates specifically to the recipes contained in this book.

Bulgur wheat
This whole wheat grain is steam-dried and cracked before sale, so only needs a brief soaking before use. Keep it cool and dry in the cupboard and it will last for a few months.

Nuts
Buy nuts in small quantities and store in a dry place. Almonds, cashews, peanuts, pecans, pine nuts and walnuts all feature prominently in this book.

Pasta
While fresh pasta is generally preferred, both for flavour and for speed of cooking, the dried product is a very valuable store cupboard ingredient. Spaghetti, noodles (Italian and oriental) and shapes are all useful.

Rice
If you stock only one type of rice, make it basmati, which has a superior flavour and fragrance. A mixture of basmati and wild rice (not a true rice, but the seeds of an aquatic grass) works well.

SPICES

Caraway seeds
Small greenish-brown seeds with a nutty texture and a flavour reminiscent of aniseed or fennel.

Chinese five-spice powder
Made from a mixture of anise pepper, cassia, fennel seed, star anise and cloves, this spice has an enticing aniseed (licorice) flavour.

Garam masala
This is an aromatic mixture of different spices used widely in Indian dishes. It is usually added at the end of cooking.

Ground cardamom
Fragrant, with a spicy undertone, cardamom is used in sweet and savoury dishes.

Ground cinnamon
A sweet fragrant spice ground from the dried rolled inner bark of a tropical tree.

Ground coriander
With a warm savoury aroma, this spice imparts a mildly hot yet sweetish flavour.

Ground cumin
Sweet and pungent, with a unique and distinctive taste.

Ground turmeric
With a somewhat musty flavour and aroma, this spice adds a deep yellow colour to food. It is sometimes used in place of saffron to add colour, although it does not have the same flavour.

Saffron
This is the most expensive spice in the world. It has a pungent scent with a slightly bitter-sweet taste. The threads are crushed and steeped in a little liquid before use.

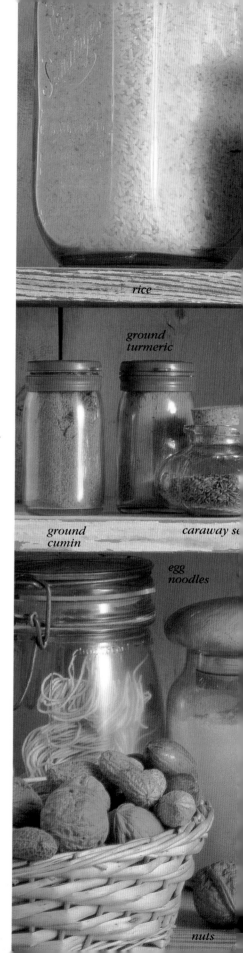

rice

ground turmeric

ground cumin

caraway se

egg noodles

nuts

penne

bulgur
wheat

pecan nuts

garam
masala

dried chillies

spaghetti

cornflour

mixed spice

black
peppercorns

Chinese five-
spice powder

pine nuts

poppy seeds

chilli
powder

ground
coriander

sea salt

thyme

cumin seed

caster sugar

long grain
rice

granulated
sugar

Fresh Produce

Beautifully fresh herbs and vegetables from around the world are readily available in our supermarkets. This vegetable checklist highlights both familiar and less well-known items.

HERBS

Basil
Well known for its affinity with tomatoes, basil has a rich spicy aroma.

Coriander
A pungent, slightly sweet herb, commonly used in Indian cooking.

Oregano
This herb has a strong flavour. It is widely used in Italian cooking.

VEGETABLES

Aubergine
A glossy oval or round vegetable, usually purple, aubergine is delicious grilled, fried or stuffed.

Chillies, red or green
Members of the capsicum (pepper) family, these are small and can be very fiery. Take care when handling chillies not to touch your eyes and mouth, as chillies contain an irritant which can sting sensitive skin.

Fennel
A bulbous leaf stalk with a distinct aniseed flavour. Fennel can be eaten raw in salads, or cooked.

Shallots
These small bulbs have a mild onion flavour and are ideal for using in sauces.

Shiitake mushrooms
An oriental mushroom with a fairly meaty scent and flavour. The stems are quite tough and are best discarded.

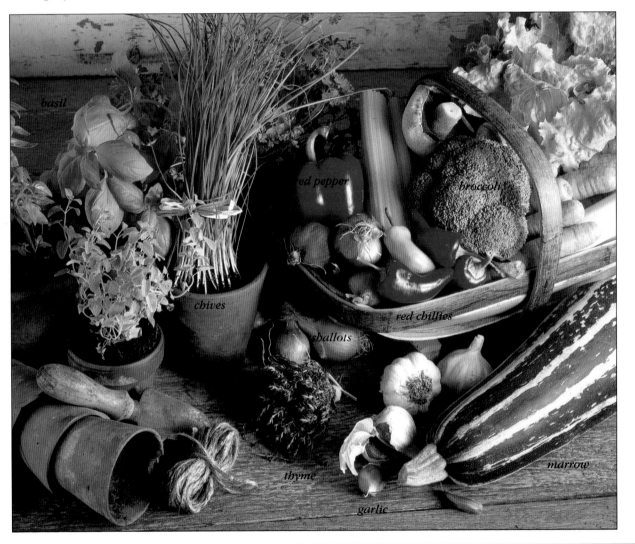

Cheeses and Tofu

Improvements in handling and distribution mean that we are now able to buy a huge range of local and imported cheeses in excellent condition. Tofu, available in various forms, is another valuable source of protein.

Blue cheese
Where a recipe fails to specify a particular blue cheese, use Roquefort if a strong flavour is required and dolcelatte for a milder result.

Camembert
This cheese is made from cow's milk. It has a mild creamy taste with a slight acidic edge that gets milder with age.

Feta
This soft Greek cheese is rindless, white in colour and has a crumbly texture. It is slightly sour, piquant and quite salty to the taste.

Goat's cheese
Fresh goat's cheese is soft and creamy. As it ages, the cheese becomes harder and the flavour intensifies.

Mozzarella
A unique Italian cheese made from cow's milk, mozzarella has a mild, creamy taste and an unusual spongy texture.

Parmesan
A hard cheese from Italy with a wonderful, distinctive flavour. It is usually grated or shaved wafer-thin. Buy it fresh as the ready-grated cheese sold commercially often lacks flavour.

Stilton
An English semi-hard cheese with blue veins, Stilton has a soft moist texture and a strong flavour.

Tofu
This is an unfermented bean curd made from soya beans. It absorbs flavours readily and is frequently marinated before use. Various forms are available, from soft silken tofu to a firm type which can be cubed and sautéed.

Equipment

Stocking up on every item in your local cookware shop will not make you a better cook, but some basic items are definitely worth investing in.

A few good saucepans in various sizes and with tight-fitting lids are a must. Heavy-based and non-stick pans are best. A large non-stick frying pan is invaluable for the quick cook. The food cooks faster when spread over a wider surface area. For the same reason, a good wok is essential. I suggest using a large saucepan or frying pan when the recipe calls for occasional stirring, and a wok for continuous movement, such as stir-frying.

Good quality knives can halve your preparation time, but more importantly, a really sharp knife is safer than a blunt one. You can do yourself a lot of damage if your hand slips when you are pressing down hard with a blunt knife. For basic, day-to-day use choose a good chopping knife, a small vegetable knife and a long serrated bread knife. If possible store knives safely in well-secured slotted racks. Drawer storage is not good for knives as the blades can easily become damaged when they are knocked around. If you do have to keep knives in a drawer, make sure they are stored with their handles towards the front for safe lifting and keep the blades protected in some way. Good sharp knives are essential and indispensable pieces of kitchen equipment, so it is worth taking care of them.

A few of the recipes in this book call for the use of a food processor, which does save time and effort but is not strictly necessary. Other essential pieces of kitchen equipment which almost seem too obvious to mention include chopping boards, a colander, a sieve, a grater, a whisk and some means of extracting citrus juice, be this a squeezer or a juicer.

For the cook who likes to cook speedily and efficiently, where you store your equipment is an important factor to consider. I use my cooker as the pivot around which most of the action takes place. Pots, pans, whisks, spoons and strainers hang conveniently overhead within easy reach, a chopping board is on an adjacent work surface and ceramic pots hold a variety of wooden spoons, spatulas, ladles, scissors, peelers and other kitchen utensils, again all within easy reach.

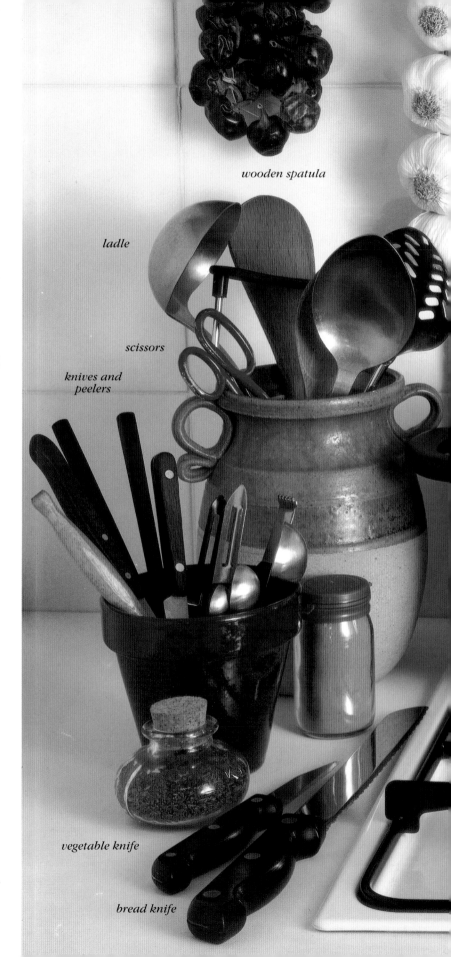

wooden spatula

ladle

scissors

knives and peelers

vegetable knife

bread knife

whisks

draining spoon

grater

serving spoon

colander

chopping board

wok

saucepans

frying pan

Make a Meal of It

The recipes in this book, although conceived as fast food, are equally suitable for entertaining. In fact, the ease and speed of preparation makes them the perfect choice when entertaining, allowing the cook more time to enjoy the company instead of being confined to the kitchen. Most of the recipes make a satisfying meal when served solo or with a simple side salad, while others may require a side order of pasta, rice or potatoes. Should you wish to serve a number of courses, I have compiled a few simple-to-make starters and desserts, followed by a selection of menus suggesting the appropriate dishes with which to serve them.

STARTERS

Lightly poached asparagus with crème fraîche and lemon.

Warm focaccia bread accompanied with olive oil, salt crystals and black olives.

Grilled cherry tomatoes served with salad and basil leaves, drizzled with a little dressing.

Crudités of celery, carrot, baby sweetcorn and mange-touts served with mayonnaise with a little pesto stirred through.

Thin slices of French bread, topped with tapenade (black olive paste) and mozzarella, then grilled and served hot.

Ready-made houmus and tzatziki served as dips with strips of warm pitta bread and black olives.

Chopped fresh tomatoes and onion flavoured with chopped fresh coriander and served with poppadums.

DESSERTS

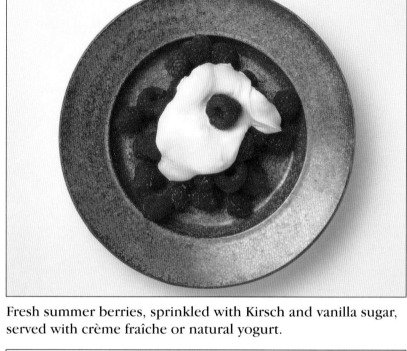

Slices of sticky ginger cake warmed through in the microwave and served with a little golden syrup and cream.

Fresh summer berries, sprinkled with Kirsch and vanilla sugar, served with crème fraîche or natural yogurt.

Sweetened whipped cream flavoured with passion fruit and served on banana slices. Add amaretti biscuits for contrast.

A slice of Swiss roll topped with a scoop of ice cream, covered in stiff meringue and grilled until golden.

Banana slices and orange segments topped with a little apricot jam, wrapped in foil and baked in a hot oven for 10 minutes. Serve with cream.

Fresh blackberries crushed lightly with a fork and gently folded into softly whipped cream. Add a drizzle of Cassis (optional) and sugar to taste.

Brandy snap baskets filled with raspberries and peach slices, topped with a swirl of cream and a sprig of mint.

Ripe plums, halved, sprinkled with brandy and filled with mascarpone cheese. The plums are topped with chopped nuts and demerara sugar then grilled until the sugar has melted.

Menus for Entertaining

When you have guests to feed, expand your 15-minute vegetarian main course into an impressive meal. The menu suggestions below feature main course 15-minute vegetarian meals accompanied by quick and easy starters, accompaniments and desserts.

Menu 1

Warm focaccia bread with salt crystals and olives

Asparagus Rolls with Herb Butter Sauce

Lentil Stir-fry served with a green salad

Summer berries with Kirsch and vanilla sugar

Menu 2

Grilled cherry tomato and basil salad

Mushrooms with Leeks and Stilton

Potato, Broccoli and Red Pepper Stir-fry

Baked banana and orange segments

Menu 3

Poached asparagus with crème fraîche and lemon

Ciabatta Rolls with Courgettes and Saffron

Red Fried Rice

Warm ginger cake with golden syrup

Menu 4

French bread slices with tapenade and mozzarella

Lemon and Parmesan Cappellini with Herb Bread

Fresh Spinach and Avocado Salad

Banana and amaretti with passion fruit cream

Menu 5

Fresh tomato and coriander with poppadoms

Bengali-style Vegetables

Cumin-spiced Marrow and Spinach

Spiced potato and cauliflower
Fresh fruit to follow

Menu 6

Crudités with mayonnaise dip

Potato, Spinach and Pine Nut Gratin

Vegetable Kebabs with Mustard and Honey

Grilled mascarpone plums

Deep-fried Courgettes with Chilli Sauce

Crunchy coated courgettes are great served with a fiery tomato sauce.

Serves 2

INGREDIENTS
15 ml/1 tbsp olive oil
1 onion, finely chopped
1 red chilli, seeded and finely diced
10 ml/2 tsp hot chilli powder
400 g/14 oz can chopped tomatoes
1 vegetable stock cube
50 ml/2 fl oz/¼ cup hot water
450 g/1 lb courgettes
150 ml/¼ pint/⅔ cup milk
50 g/2 oz/½ cup plain flour
oil for deep-frying
salt and freshly ground black pepper
thyme sprigs, to garnish

TO SERVE
lettuce leaves
watercress sprigs
slices of seeded bread

courgettes
chopped tomatoes
onion
red chilli
plain flour
stock cube
milk
chilli powder

1 Heat the oil in a pan. Add the onion and cook for 2–3 minutes. Add the chilli. Stir in the chilli powder and cook for 30 seconds.

2 Add the tomatoes. Crumble in the stock cube and stir in the water. Cover and cook for 10 minutes.

3 Meanwhile, top and tail the courgettes. Cut into 5 mm/¼ in slices.

4 Pour the milk into one shallow dish and spread out the flour in another. Dip the courgettes first in the milk, then into the flour, until well-coated.

5 Heat the oil for deep-frying to 180°C/350°F or until a cube of bread, when added to the oil, browns in 30–45 seconds. Add the courgettes in batches and deep-fry for 3–4 minutes until crisp. Drain on kitchen paper.

6 Place two or three lettuce leaves on each serving plate. Add a few sprigs of watercress and fan out the bread slices to one side. Season the sauce, spoon some on to each plate, top with the crisp courgettes and garnish with the thyme sprigs. Serve at once with salad and bread.

Cumin-spiced Marrow and Spinach

Tender chunks of marrow with spinach in a creamy, cumin-flavoured sauce.

Serves 2

INGREDIENTS

¹/₂ marrow, about 450 g/1 lb
30 ml/2 tbsp vegetable oil
10 ml/2 tsp cumin seeds
1 small red chilli, seeded and
  finely chopped
30 ml/2 tbsp water
50 g/2 oz tender young
  spinach leaves
90 ml/6 tbsp single cream
salt and freshly ground black pepper

spinach leaves

cumin seeds

marrow

single cream

red chilli

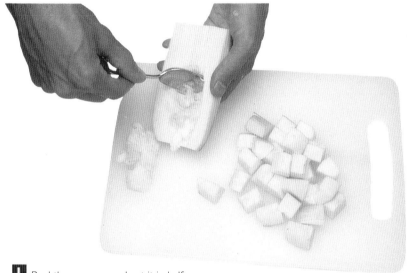

1 Peel the marrow and cut it in half. Scoop out the seeds. Cut the flesh into cubes.

2 Heat the oil in a large frying pan. Add the cumin seeds and the chopped chilli. Cook for 1 minute.

3 Add the marrow and water to the pan. Cover with foil or a lid and simmer for 8 minutes, stirring occasionally, until the marrow is just tender. Remove the cover and cook for 2 minutes more or until most of the water has evaporated.

4 Put the spinach leaves in a colander. Rinse well under cold water, drain and pat dry with kitchen paper. Tear into rough pieces.

5 Add the spinach to the marrow, replace the cover and cook gently for 1 minute. Serve hot.

COOK'S TIP
Be careful when handling chillies as the juice can burn sensitive skin. Wear rubber gloves or wash hands thoroughly after preparation.

6 Stir in the cream and cook over a high heat for 2 minutes. Add salt and pepper to taste, and serve. An Indian rice dish would be a good accompaniment. Alternatively, serve with naan bread.

Chilli Beans with Basmati Rice

Red kidney beans, tomatoes and chilli make a great combination. Serve with pasta or pitta bread instead of rice, if you prefer.

Serves 4

INGREDIENTS
350 g/12 oz/2 cups basmati rice
30 ml/2 tbsp olive oil
1 large onion, chopped
1 garlic clove, crushed
15 ml/1 tbsp hot chilli powder
15 ml/1 tbsp plain flour
15 ml/1 tbsp tomato purée
400 g/14 oz can chopped tomatoes
400 g/14 oz can red kidney
  beans, drained
150 ml/¼ pint/⅔ cup hot
  vegetable stock
chopped fresh parsley, to garnish
salt and freshly ground black pepper

basmati rice

chopped tomatoes

chilli powder

onion

tomato purée

garlic clove

stock cube

red kidney beans

plain flour

1 Wash the rice several times under cold running water. Drain well. Bring a large pan of water to the boil. Add the rice and cook for 10–12 minutes, until tender. Meanwhile, heat the oil in a frying pan. Add the onion and garlic and cook for 2 minutes.

2 Stir the chilli powder and flour into the onion and garlic mixture. Cook for 2 minutes, stirring frequently.

3 Stir in the tomato purée and chopped tomatoes. Rinse the kidney beans under cold water, drain well and add to the pan with the hot vegetable stock. Cover and cook for 12 minutes, stirring occasionally.

4 Season the chilli sauce with salt and pepper. Drain the rice and serve at once, with the chilli beans, sprinkled with a little chopped fresh parsley.

Spicy Cauliflower and Potato Salad

A delicious cold vegetable salad with a hot spicy dressing.

Serves 2–3

INGREDIENTS
1 medium cauliflower
2 medium potatoes
7.5 ml/1½ tsp caraway seeds
5 ml/1 tsp ground coriander
2.5 ml/½ tsp hot chilli powder
juice of 1 lemon
60 ml/4 tbsp olive oil
salt and freshly ground black pepper

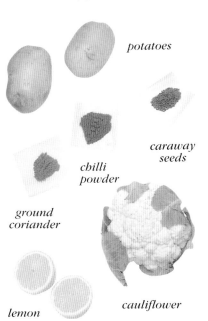

potatoes

caraway seeds

chilli powder

ground coriander

lemon

cauliflower

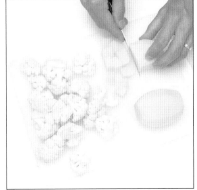

1 Break the cauliflower into small florets. Peel the potatoes and cut them into chunks.

2 Bring a large pan of water to the boil. Add the cauliflower florets and potato chunks and cook for 8 minutes until just tender.

3 Meanwhile, heat a non-stick frying pan. Add the caraway seeds and fry, shaking the pan constantly, for 1 minute. Tip the roasted seeds into a bowl and add the ground coriander and chilli powder, with salt and pepper to taste. Stir in the lemon juice and olive oil and mix to a paste.

4 Drain the vegetables well. Add them to the bowl and toss to coat in the chilli dressing. Serve at once, with hot pitta bread or brown rice.

Bengali-style Vegetables

A hot dry curry using spices that do not require long slow cooking.

Serves 4

INGREDIENTS

¹/₂ medium cauliflower, broken into
  small florets
1 large potato, peeled and cut into
  2.5 cm/1 in dice
115 g/4 oz French beans, trimmed
2 courgettes, halved lengthways
  and sliced
2 green chillies
2.5 cm/1 in piece of fresh root
  ginger, peeled
120 ml/4 fl oz/¹/₂ cup natural yogurt
10 ml/2 tsp ground coriander
2.5 ml/¹/₂ tsp ground turmeric
25 g/1 oz/2 tbsp ghee
2.5 ml/¹/₂ tsp garam masala
5 ml/1 tsp cumin seeds
10 ml/2 tsp sugar
pinch each of ground cloves,
  ground cinnamon and
    ground cardamom
salt and freshly ground black pepper

1 Bring a large pan of water to the boil. Add the cauliflower and potato and cook for 5 minutes. Add the beans and courgettes and cook for 2–3 minutes.

2 Meanwhile, cut the chillies in half, remove the seeds and roughly chop the flesh. Finely chop the ginger. Mix the chillies and ginger in a small bowl.

green chilli

cumin seeds

French beans

root ginger

cauliflower florets

natural yogurt

potato

sugar

ground turmeric

courgettes

ghee

ground cinnamon

ground coriander

ground cloves

garam masala

3 Drain the vegetables and tip them into a bowl. Add the chilli and ginger mixture, with the yogurt, ground coriander and turmeric. Season with plenty of salt and pepper and mix well.

4 Heat the ghee in a large frying pan. Add the vegetable mixture and cook over a high heat for 2 minutes, stirring from time to time.

5 Stir in the garam masala and cumin seeds and cook for 2 minutes.

6 Stir in the sugar and remaining spices and cook for 1 minute or until all the liquid has evaporated.

COOK'S TIP

If ghee is not available you can clarify your own butter. Melt 50 g/2 oz/¼ cup butter slowly in a small pan. Remove from the heat and leave for about 5 minutes. Pour off the clear yellow clarified butter, leaving the sediment in the pan.

Vegetable Fajita

A colourful medley of mushrooms and peppers in a spicy sauce, wrapped in tortillas and served with creamy guacamole.

Serves 2

INGREDIENTS
1 onion
1 red pepper
1 green pepper
1 yellow pepper
1 garlic clove, crushed
225 g/8 oz mushrooms
90 ml/6 tbsp vegetable oil
30 ml/2 tbsp medium chilli powder
salt and freshly ground black pepper
coriander sprigs and 1 lime, cut into
   wedges, to garnish

FOR THE GUACAMOLE
1 ripe avocado
1 shallot, roughly chopped
1 green chilli, seeded and
   roughly chopped
juice of 1 lime

TO SERVE
4–6 flour tortillas, warmed

green
pepper

*yellow
pepper*

red pepper

mushrooms

green chilli

*garlic
clove*

shallot

avocado

lime

chilli powder

onion

1 Slice the onion. Cut the peppers in half, remove the seeds and cut the flesh into strips. Combine the onion and peppers in a bowl. Add the crushed garlic and mix lightly.

2 Remove the mushroom stalks. Save for making stock, or discard. Slice the mushroom caps and add to the pepper mixture in the bowl. Mix the oil and chilli powder in a cup, pour over the vegetable mixture and stir well. Set aside.

3 Make the guacamole. Cut the avocado in half and remove the stone and the peel. Put the flesh into a food processor or blender with the shallot, green chilli and lime juice. Process for 1 minute until smooth. Scrape into a small bowl, cover closely and put in the fridge to chill until required.

4 Heat a frying pan or wok until very hot. Add the marinated vegetables and stir-fry over high heat for 5–6 minutes until the mushrooms and pepper are just tender. Season well. Spoon a little of the filling on to each tortilla and roll up. Garnish with fresh coriander and lime wedges and serve with the guacamole.

Curried Eggs

Hard-boiled eggs are served on a bed of mild creamy sauce with a hint of curry.

Serves 2

INGREDIENTS

4 eggs
15 ml/1 tbsp sunflower oil
1 small onion, finely chopped
2.5 cm/1 in piece of fresh root
  ginger, peeled and grated
2.5 ml/¹/₂ tsp ground cumin
2.5 ml/¹/₂ tsp garam masala
25 ml/1¹/₂ tbsp tomato purée
10 ml/2 tsp tandoori paste
10 ml/2 tsp lemon juice
50 ml/2 fl oz/¹/₄ cup single cream
15 ml/1 tbsp chopped
  fresh coriander
salt and freshly ground black pepper
coriander sprigs, to garnish

fresh coriander

eggs *root ginger* *garam masala*

ground cumin *single cream*

tomato purée *lemon*

tandoori paste *onion*

1 Put the eggs in a pan of water. Bring to the boil, lower the heat and simmer for 10 minutes.

2 Meanwhile, heat the oil in a frying pan. Cook the onion for 2–3 minutes. Add the ginger and cook for 1 minute.

3 Stir in the ground cumin, garam masala, tomato purée, tandoori paste, lemon juice and cream. Cook for 1–2 minutes, then stir in the coriander. Add salt and pepper to taste.

4 Drain the eggs, remove the shells and cut each egg in half. Spoon the sauce into a serving bowl, top with the eggs and garnish with the fresh coriander. Serve at once.

Breaded Aubergine with Hot Vinaigrette

Crisp on the outside, beautifully tender within, these aubergine slices taste wonderful with a spicy dressing flavoured with chilli and capers.

Serves 2

INGREDIENTS
1 large aubergine
50 g/2 oz/¹/₂ cup plain flour
2 eggs, beaten
115 g/4 oz/2 cups fresh
  white breadcrumbs
vegetable oil for frying
1 head radicchio
salt and freshly ground black pepper

FOR THE DRESSING
30 ml/2 tbsp olive oil
1 garlic clove, crushed
15 ml/1 tbsp capers, drained
15 ml/1 tbsp white wine vinegar
15 ml/1 tbsp chilli oil

aubergine

breadcrumbs

eggs

plain flour

radicchio

capers

white wine vinegar

garlic clove

COOK'S TIP
When serving a salad with a warm dressing use robust leaves that will stand up to the heat.

1 Top and tail the aubergine. Cut it into 5 mm/¹/₄ in slices. Set aside.

2 Season the flour with a generous amount of salt and black pepper. Spread out in a shallow dish. Pour the beaten eggs into a second dish, and spread out the breadcrumbs in a third.

3 Dip the aubergine slices in the flour, then in the beaten egg and finally in the breadcrumbs, patting them on to make an even coating.

4 Pour vegetable oil into a large frying pan to a depth of about 5 mm/¹/₄ in. Heat the oil, then fry the aubergine slices for 3–4 minutes, turning once. Drain on kitchen paper.

5 Heat the olive oil in a small pan. Add the garlic and the capers and cook over gentle heat for 1 minute. Increase the heat, add the vinegar and cook for 30 seconds. Stir in the chilli oil and remove the pan from the heat.

6 Arrange the radicchio leaves on two plates. Top with the hot aubergine slices. Drizzle over the vinaigrette and serve.

Double Tomato Tagliatelle

Sun-dried tomatoes add pungency to this dish, while the grilled fresh tomatoes add bite.

Serves 4

INGREDIENTS
45 ml/3 tbsp olive oil
1 garlic clove, crushed
1 small onion, chopped
50 ml/2 fl oz/¼ cup dry white wine
6 sun-dried tomatoes, chopped
30 ml/2 tbsp chopped fresh parsley
50 g/2 oz/½ cup stoned black
  olives, halved
450 g/1 lb fresh tagliatelle
4 tomatoes, halved
Parmesan cheese, to serve
salt and freshly ground black pepper

tomatoes

parsley

garlic clove

sun-dried tomatoes

tagliatelle

dry white wine

onion

black olives

Parmesan cheese

COOK'S TIP

It is essential to buy Parmesan in a piece for this dish. Find a good source – fresh Parmesan should not be unacceptably hard – and shave or grate it yourself. The flavour will be much more intense than that of the ready-grated product.

1 Heat 30 ml/2 tbsp of the oil in a pan. Add the garlic and onion and cook for 2–3 minutes, stirring occasionally. Add the wine, sun-dried tomatoes and the parsley. Cook for 2 minutes. Stir in the black olives.

2 Bring a large pan of salted water to the boil. Add the fresh tagliatelle and cook for 2–3 minutes until just tender. Preheat the grill.

3 Put the tomatoes on a tray and brush with the remaining oil. Grill for 3–4 minutes.

4 Drain the pasta, return it to the pan and toss with the sauce. Serve with the grilled tomatoes, freshly ground black pepper and shavings of Parmesan.

Penne with Fennel Concassé and Blue Cheese

The aniseed flavour of the fennel makes it the perfect partner for tomato, especially when topped with blue cheese.

Serves 2

INGREDIENTS
1 fennel bulb
225 g/8 oz penne or other dried
  pasta shapes
30 ml/2 tbsp extra virgin olive oil
1 shallot, finely chopped
300 ml/^{1}/$_2$ pint/1^1/$_4$ cups passata
pinch of sugar
5 ml/1 tsp chopped fresh oregano
115 g/4 oz blue cheese
salt and freshly ground black pepper

oregano

shallot

fennel bulb

penne

passata

sugar

blue cheese

1 Cut the fennel bulb in half. Cut away the hard core and root. Slice the fennel thinly, then cut the slices into strips.

2 Bring a large pan of salted water to the boil. Add the pasta and cook for 10–12 minutes until just tender.

3 Meanwhile, heat the oil in a small saucepan. Add the fennel and shallot and cook for 2–3 minutes over a high heat, stirring occasionally.

4 Add the passata, sugar and oregano. Cover the pan and simmer gently for 10–12 minutes, until the fennel is tender. Add salt and pepper to taste. Drain the pasta and return it to the pan and toss with the sauce. Serve in bowls, with the blue cheese crumbled over the top.

Lemon and Parmesan Capellini with Herb Bread

Cream is thickened with Parmesan and flavoured with lemon to make a superb sauce for pasta.

Serves 2

INGREDIENTS

½ Granary baguette
50 g/2 oz/¼ cup butter, softened
1 garlic clove, crushed
30 ml/2 tbsp chopped fresh herbs
225 g/8 oz dried or fresh capellini
250 ml/8 fl oz/1 cup single cream
75 g/3 oz Parmesan cheese, grated
finely grated rind of 1 lemon
salt and freshly ground black pepper

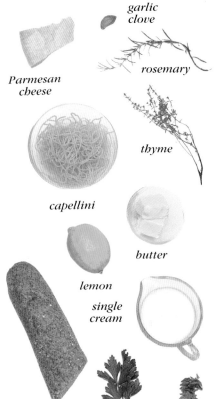

garlic clove

Parmesan cheese

rosemary

thyme

capellini

butter

lemon

single cream

Granary baguette   *parsley*   *oregano*

1 Preheat the oven to 200°C/400°F/ Gas 6. Cut the baguette into thick slices.

2 Put the butter in a bowl and beat with the garlic and herbs. Spread thickly over each slice of bread.

3 Reassemble the baguette. Wrap in foil, support on a baking sheet and bake for 10 minutes.

4 Meanwhile, bring a large pan of water to the boil and cook the pasta until just tender. Dried pasta will take 10–12 minutes; fresh pasta will be ready in 2–3 minutes.

5 Pour the cream into another pan and bring to the boil. Stir in the Parmesan and lemon rind. The sauce should thicken in about 30 seconds.

6 Drain the pasta, return it to the pan and toss with the sauce. Season to taste and sprinkle with a little chopped fresh parsley and grated lemon rind, if liked. Serve with the hot herb bread.

Summer Pasta Salad

Tender young vegetables in a light dressing make a delicious lunch.

Serves 2–3

INGREDIENTS

225 g/8 oz fusilli or other dried
  pasta shapes
115 g/4 oz baby carrots, trimmed
  and halved
115 g/4 oz baby sweetcorn, halved
  lengthways
50 g/2 oz mange-touts
115 g/4 oz young asparagus
  spears, trimmed
4 spring onions, trimmed
  and shredded
10 ml/2 tsp white wine vinegar
60 ml/4 tbsp extra virgin olive oil
15 ml/1 tbsp wholegrain mustard
salt and freshly ground black pepper

spring onions

young asparagus

fusilli

baby carrots

wholegrain mustard

baby sweetcorn

white wine vinegar

mange-touts

1 Bring a large pan of salted water to the boil. Add the pasta and cook for 10–12 minutes, until just tender. Meanwhile, cook the carrots and sweetcorn in a second pan of boiling salted water for 5 minutes.

2 Add the mange-touts and asparagus to the carrot mixture and cook for 2–3 minutes more. Drain all the vegetables and refresh under cold running water. Drain again.

3 Tip the vegetable mixture into a mixing bowl, add the spring onions and toss well together.

4 Drain the pasta, refresh it under cold running water and drain again. Toss with the vegetables. Mix the vinegar, olive oil and mustard in a jar. Add salt and pepper to taste, close the jar tightly and shake well. Pour the dressing over the salad. Toss well and serve.

Five-spice Vegetable Noodles

Vary this vegetable stir-fry by substituting mushrooms, bamboo shoots, beansprouts, mange-touts or water chestnuts for some or all of the vegetables suggested below.

Serves 2–3

INGREDIENTS
225 g/8 oz dried egg noodles
30 ml/2 tbsp sesame oil
2 carrots
1 celery stick
1 small fennel bulb
2 courgettes, halved and sliced
1 red chilli, seeded and chopped
2.5 cm/1 in piece of fresh root
  ginger, peeled and grated
1 garlic clove, crushed
7.5 ml/1$\frac{1}{2}$ tsp Chinese five-spice
  powder
2.5 ml/$\frac{1}{2}$ tsp ground cinnamon
4 spring onions, sliced
50 ml/2 fl oz/$\frac{1}{4}$ cup warm water

carrots
celery stick
garlic clove
fennel bulb
egg noodles
courgettes
five-spice powder
spring onions
cinnamon
root ginger

1 Bring a large pan of salted water to the boil. Add the noodles and cook for 2–3 minutes until just tender. Drain the noodles, return them to the pan and toss in a little of the oil. Set aside.

2 Cut the carrot and celery into julienne. Cut the fennel bulb in half and cut out the hard core. Cut into slices, then cut the slices into julienne.

3 Heat the remaining oil in a wok or frying pan until very hot. Add all the vegetables, including the chilli, and stir-fry for 7–8 minutes.

4 Add the ginger and garlic and stir-fry for 2 minutes, then add the spices. Cook for 1 minute. Add the spring onions and stir-fry for 1 minute. Pour in the warm water and cook for 1 minute. Stir in the noodles and toss well together. Serve sprinkled with sliced red chilli, if liked.

Mushroom Bolognese

A quick – and exceedingly tasty – vegetarian
version of the classic Italian meat dish.

Serves 4

INGREDIENTS
450 g/1 lb mushrooms
15 ml/1 tbsp olive oil
1 onion, chopped
1 garlic clove, crushed
15 ml/1 tbsp tomato purée
400 g/14 oz can chopped tomatoes
15 ml/1 tbsp chopped fresh oregano
450 g/1 lb fresh pasta
Parmesan cheese, to serve
chopped fresh oregano, to garnish

mushrooms

chopped tomatoes

oregano

pasta

garlic clove

onion

Parmesan cheese

tomato purée

1 Trim the mushroom stems neatly,
then cut each mushroom into quarters.

2 Heat the oil in a large pan. Add the
chopped onion and garlic and cook for
2–3 minutes.

3 Add the mushrooms to the pan and
cook over a high heat for 3–4 minutes,
stirring occasionally.

4 Stir in the tomato purée, chopped
tomatoes and oregano. Lower the heat,
cover and cook for 5 minutes.

5 Meanwhile, bring a large pan of
salted water to the boil. Cook the pasta
for 2–3 minutes until just tender.

COOK'S TIP

If you prefer to use dried pasta, make this the first thing that you cook. It will take 10–12 minutes, during which time you can make the mushroom mixture. Use 350 g/12 oz dried pasta.

6 Season the bolognese sauce with salt and pepper. Drain the pasta, tip it into a bowl and add the mushroom mixture. Toss to mix. Serve in individual bowls, topped with shavings of fresh Parmesan cheese and a sprinkling of chopped fresh oregano.

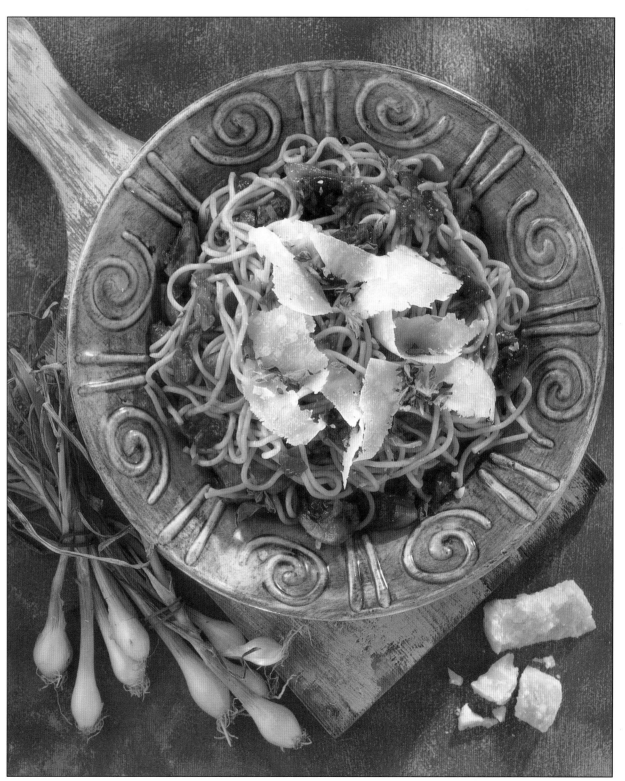

Fried Noodles with Beansprouts and Asparagus

Soft fried noodles contrast beautifully with crisp beansprouts and asparagus.

Serves 2

INGREDIENTS
115 g/4 oz dried egg noodles
60 ml/4 tbsp vegetable oil
1 small onion, chopped
2.5 cm/1 in piece of fresh root
  ginger, peeled and grated
2 garlic cloves, crushed
175 g/6 oz young asparagus
  spears, trimmed
115 g/4 oz beansprouts
4 spring onions, sliced
45 ml/3 tbsp soy sauce
salt and freshly ground black pepper

onion

spring onions

garlic cloves

root ginger

soy sauce

egg noodles

beansprouts

asparagus spears

1 Bring a pan of salted water to the boil. Add the noodles and cook for 2–3 minutes, until just tender. Drain and toss in 30 ml/2 tbsp of the oil.

2 Heat the remaining oil in a wok or frying pan until very hot. Add the onion, ginger and garlic and stir-fry for 2–3 minutes. Add the asparagus and stir-fry for a further 2–3 minutes.

3 Add the noodles and beansprouts and stir-fry for 2 minutes.

4 Stir in the spring onions and soy sauce. Season to taste, adding salt sparingly as the soy sauce will add quite a salty flavour. Stir-fry for 1 minute, then serve at once.

Pasta with Coriander and Grilled Aubergines

Pasta with a piquant sauce of coriander and lime – a variation on the classic pesto – is superb served with grilled aubergines.

Serves 2

INGREDIENTS
15 g/¹/₂ oz coriander leaves
30 ml/2 tbsp pine nuts
30 ml/2 tbsp freshly grated
  Parmesan cheese
3 garlic cloves
juice of ¹/₂ lime
105 ml/7 tbsp olive oil
225 g/8 oz dried cellentani or other
  pasta shapes
1 large aubergine
salt and freshly ground black pepper

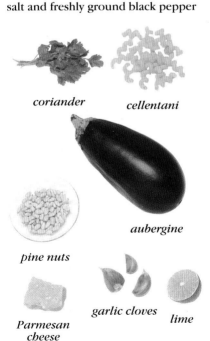

coriander *cellentani*

aubergine

pine nuts

Parmesan cheese *garlic cloves* *lime*

1 Process the coriander leaves, pine nuts, Parmesan, garlic, lime juice and 60 ml/4 tbsp of the olive oil in a food processor or blender for 30 seconds until almost smooth. Bring a pan of salted water to the boil, add the pasta and cook for 10–12 minutes until cooked but firm to the bite.

2 Meanwhile, cut the aubergine in half lengthways, then cut each half into 5 mm/¹/₄ in slices. Spread out on a baking sheet, brush with the remaining oil and season well with salt and black pepper.

3 Grill the aubergine slices for about 4 minutes. Turn them over and brush with the remaining oil. Season as before. Grill for 4 minutes more.

4 Drain the pasta, tip it into a bowl and toss with the coriander sauce. Serve with the grilled aubergine slices.

Parmesan and Poached Egg Salad with Croûtons

Soft poached eggs, hot garlic croûtons and cool, crisp salad leaves make an unforgettable combination.

Serves 2

INGREDIENTS

$^{1}/_{2}$ small loaf white bread
75 ml/5 tbsp extra virgin olive oil
2 eggs
115 g/4 oz mixed salad leaves
2 garlic cloves, crushed
7.5 ml/$^{1}/_{2}$ tbsp white wine vinegar
25 g/1 oz Parmesan cheese

Parmesan cheese

mixed salad leaves

white bread

garlic cloves

eggs

1 Remove the crust from the bread. Cut the bread into 2.5 cm/1 in cubes.

2 Heat 30 ml/2 tbsp of the oil in a frying pan. Cook the bread for about 5 minutes, tossing the cubes occasionally, until they are golden brown.

3 Meanwhile, bring a pan of water to the boil. Carefully slide in the eggs, one at a time. Gently poach the eggs for 4 minutes until lightly cooked.

4 Divide the salad leaves between two plates. Remove the croûtons from the pan and arrange them over the leaves. Wipe the pan clean with kitchen paper.

5 Heat the remaining oil in the pan, add the garlic and vinegar and cook over high heat for 1 minute. Pour the warm dressing over each salad.

COOK'S TIP

Add a dash of vinegar to the water before poaching the eggs. This helps to keep the whites together. To ensure that a poached egg has a good shape, swirl the water with a spoon, whirlpool-fashion, before sliding in the egg.

6 Place a poached egg on each salad. Scatter with shavings of Parmesan and a little freshly ground black pepper, if liked.

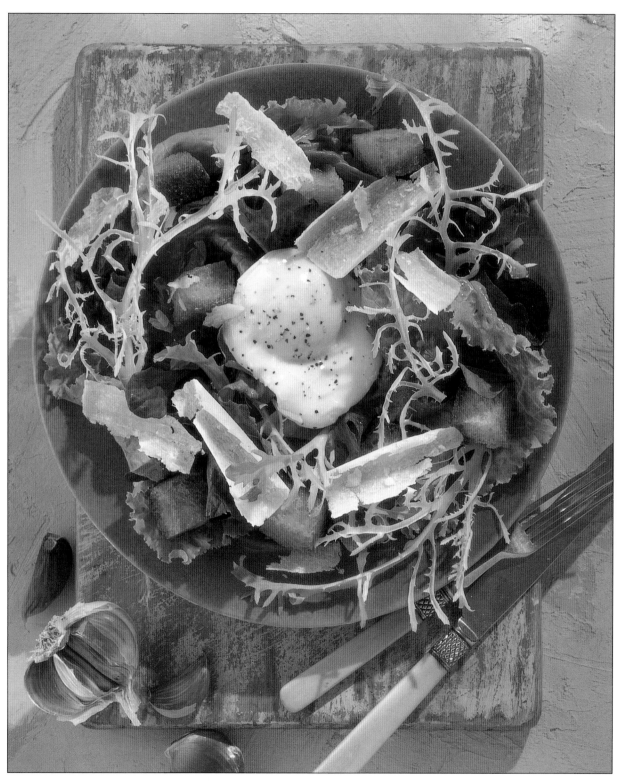

Classic Greek Salad

If you have ever visited Greece you'll know that a Greek salad with a chunk of bread makes a delicious, filling meal.

Serves 4

INGREDIENTS

1 cos lettuce
½ cucumber, halved lengthways
4 tomatoes
8 spring onions
75 g/3 oz/2½ cups Greek
  black olives
115 g/4 oz feta cheese
90 ml/6 tbsp white wine vinegar
150 ml/¼ pint/⅔ cup extra virgin
  olive oil
salt and freshly ground black pepper

cos lettuce

tomatoes

feta cheese

black olives

white wine vinegar

cucumber

spring onions

COOK'S TIP
The salad can be assembled in advance and chilled, but should only be dressed just before serving. Keep the dressing at room temperature as chilling deadens its flavour.

1 Tear the lettuce leaves into pieces and place them in a large mixing bowl. Slice the cucumber and add to the bowl.

2 Cut the tomatoes into wedges and put them into the bowl.

3 Slice the spring onions. Add them to the bowl with the olives and toss well.

4 Cut the feta cheese into cubes and add to the salad.

5 Put the vinegar, olive oil and seasoning into a small bowl and whisk well. Pour the dressing over the salad and toss to combine. Serve at once, with extra olives and chunks of bread, if liked.

Chicory, Fruit and Nut Salad

Mildly bitter chicory is wonderful with sweet fruit, and is especially delicious when complemented by a creamy curry sauce.

Serves 4

INGREDIENTS

45 ml/3 tbsp mayonnaise
15 ml/1 tbsp Greek yogurt
15 ml/1 tbsp mild curry paste
90 ml/6 tbsp single cream
$^1/_2$ iceberg lettuce
2 heads of chicory
50 g/2 oz/$^1/_2$ cup cashew nuts
50 g/2 oz/$1^1/_4$ cups flaked coconut
2 red apples
75 g/3 oz/$^1/_2$ cup currants

currants

iceberg lettuce

cashew nuts   *curry paste*   *mayonnaise*

red apples

single cream   *flaked coconut*

chicory

1 Mix the mayonnaise, Greek yogurt, curry paste and single cream in a small bowl. Cover and chill until required.

2 Tear the iceberg lettuce into pieces and put into a mixing bowl.

3 Cut the root end off each head of chicory, separate the leaves and add them to the lettuce. Preheat the grill.

4 Toast the cashew nuts for 2 minutes until golden. Tip into a bowl and set aside. Spread out the coconut flakes on a baking sheet. Grill for 1 minute until golden.

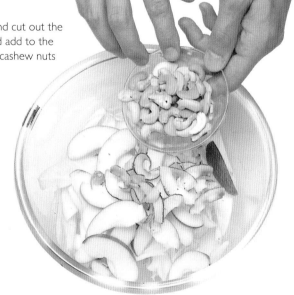

5 Quarter the apples and cut out the cores. Slice the apples and add to the lettuce with the coconut, cashew nuts and currants.

COOK'S TIP
Watch the coconut and cashew nuts very carefully when grilling, as they brown very fast.

6 Spoon the dressing over the salad, toss lightly and serve.

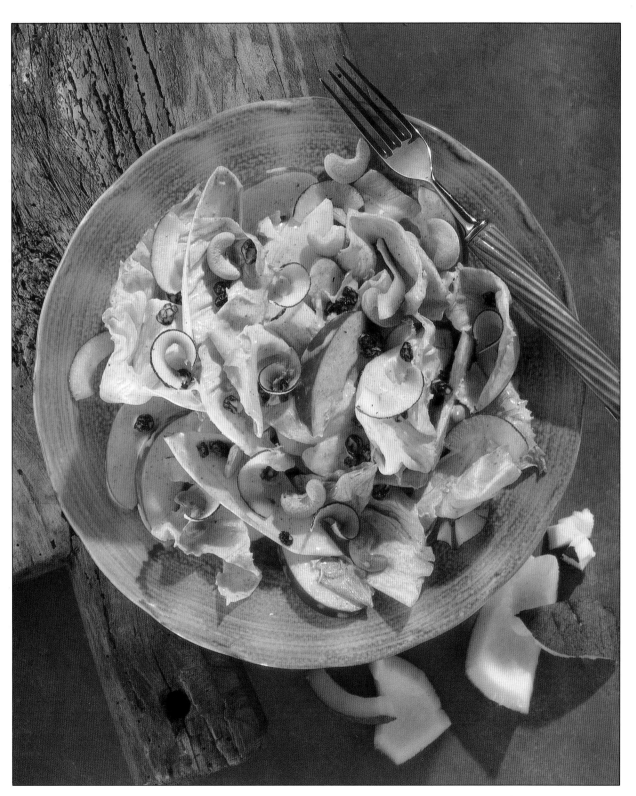

Grilled Pepper Salad

Grilled peppers are delicious served hot with a sharp dressing. You can also serve them cold.

Serves 2

INGREDIENTS
1 red pepper
1 green pepper
1 yellow or orange pepper
¹/₂ radicchio, separated into leaves
¹/₂ frisée, separated into leaves
7.5 ml/1¹/₂ tsp white wine vinegar
30 ml/2 tbsp extra virgin olive oil
175 g/6 oz goat's cheese
salt and freshly ground black pepper

frisée

red pepper

green pepper

yellow pepper

goat's cheese

white wine vinegar

radicchio

1 Preheat the grill. Cut all the peppers in half. Cut each half into pieces.

2 Put the pepper pieces on a rack set over a grill pan. Grill for 10 minutes.

3 Meanwhile, divide the radicchio and frisée leaves between two plates. Chill until required.

4 Mix the vinegar and olive oil in a jar. Add salt and pepper to taste, close the jar tightly and shake well.

5 Slice the goat's cheese, place on a baking sheet and grill for 1 minute.

6 Arrange the peppers and grilled goat's cheese on the salads. Pour over the dressing and grind a little extra black pepper over each.

COOK'S TIP
Grill the peppers until they just start to blacken around the edges – don't let them burn.

Courgettes, Carrots and Pecans in Pitta Bread

Chunks of fried courgette served with a tangy salad in pitta pockets.

Serves 2

INGREDIENTS
2 carrots
25 g/1 oz/¹/₄ cup pecan nuts
4 spring onions, sliced
50 ml/2 fl oz/¹/₄ cup Greek yogurt
35 ml/7 tsp olive oil
5 ml/1 tsp lemon juice
15 ml/1 tbsp chopped fresh mint
2 courgettes
25 g/1 oz/¹/₄ cup plain flour
2 pitta breads
salt and freshly ground black pepper
shredded lettuce, to serve

courgettes

spring onions

pecan nuts *lemon*

mint

Greek yogurt

carrots

1 Top and tail the carrots. Grate them coarsely into a bowl.

2 Stir in the pecans and spring onions and toss well.

3 In a clean bowl, whisk the yogurt with 7.5 ml/1¹/₂ tsp of the olive oil, the lemon juice and the fresh mint. Stir the dressing into the carrot mixture and mix well. Cover and chill until required.

4 Top and tail the courgettes. Cut them diagonally into slices. Season the flour with salt and pepper. Spread it out on a plate and coat the courgette slices.

COOK'S TIP
Do not fill the pitta breads too soon or the carrot mixture will make the bread soggy.

5 Heat the remaining oil in a large frying pan. Add the coated courgette slices and cook for 3–4 minutes, turning once, until browned. Drain the courgettes on kitchen paper.

6 Make a slit in each pitta bread to form a pocket. Fill the pittas with the carrot mixture and the courgette slices. Serve on a bed of shredded lettuce.

Courgette Puffs with Salad and Balsamic Dressing

This unusual salad consists of deep-fried courgettes, flavoured with mint and served warm on a bed of salad leaves with a balsamic dressing.

Serves 2

INGREDIENTS
450 g/1 lb courgettes
75 g/3 oz/1½ cups fresh white
  breadcrumbs
1 egg
pinch of cayenne pepper
15 ml/1 tbsp chopped fresh mint
oil for deep-frying
15 ml/1 tbsp/3 tbsp balsamic vinegar
45 ml/3 tbsp extra virgin olive oil
200 g/7 oz mixed salad leaves
salt and freshly ground black pepper

courgettes

white breadcrumbs

balsamic vinegar

mixed salad leaves

egg   *mint*

1 Top and tail the courgettes. Coarsely grate them and put into a colander. Squeeze out the excess water, then put the courgettes into a bowl.

2 Add the breadcrumbs, egg, cayenne, mint and seasoning. Mix well.

3 Shape the courgette mixture into balls, about the size of walnuts.

4 Heat the oil for deep-frying to 180°C/350°F or until a cube of bread, when added to the oil, browns in 30–40 seconds. Deep-fry the courgette balls in batches for 2–3 minutes. Drain on kitchen paper.

5 Whisk the vinegar and oil together and season well.

6 Put the salad leaves in a bowl and pour over the dressing. Add the courgette puffs and toss lightly together. Serve at once, while the courgette puffs are still crisp.

Vegetable and Satay Salad

Baby new potatoes, tender vegetables and crunchy chick-peas are smothered in a creamy peanut dressing.

Serves 4

INGREDIENTS
450 g/1 lb baby new potatoes
1 small head cauliflower, broken
  into small florets
225 g/8 oz French beans, trimmed
400 g/14 oz can chick-peas, drained
115 g/4 oz watercress sprigs
115 g/4 oz beansprouts
8 spring onions, sliced
60 ml/4 tbsp crunchy peanut butter
150 ml/¼ pint/⅔ cup hot water
5 ml/1 tsp chilli sauce
10 ml/2 tsp soft brown sugar
5 ml/1 tsp soy sauce
5 ml/1 tsp lime juice

cauliflower

watercress

soy sauce

spring onions

crunchy peanut butter

soft brown sugar

chick-peas

beansprouts

chilli sauce

French beans

lime

baby new potatoes

1 Put the potatoes into a pan and add water to just cover. Bring to the boil and cook for 10–12 minutes or until the potatoes are just tender when pierced with the point of a sharp knife. Drain and refresh under cold running water. Drain once again.

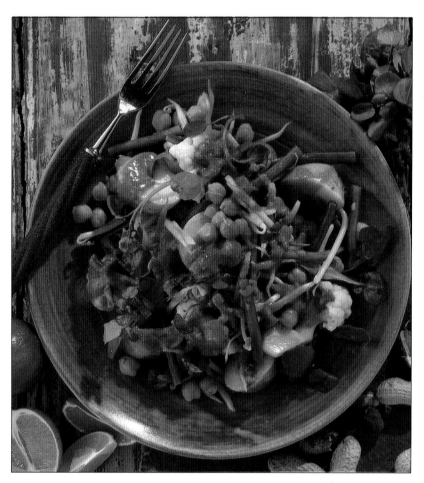

2 Meanwhile, bring another pan of salted water to the boil. Add the cauliflower and cook for 5 minutes, then add the beans and cook for 5 minutes more. Drain both vegetables, refresh under cold water and drain again.

3 Put the cauliflower and beans into a large bowl and add the chick-peas. Halve the potatoes and add. Toss lightly. Mix the watercress, beansprouts and spring onions together. Divide between four plates and pile the vegetables on top.

4 Put the peanut butter into a bowl and stir in the water. Add the chilli sauce, brown sugar, soy sauce and lime juice. Whisk well then drizzle the dressing over the vegetables.

Fresh Spinach and Avocado Salad

Young tender spinach leaves make a change from lettuce and are delicious served with avocado, cherry tomatoes and radishes in a tofu sauce.

Serves 2-3

INGREDIENTS
1 large avocado
juice of 1 lime
225 g/8 oz fresh baby spinach leaves
115 g/4 oz cherry tomatoes
4 spring onions, sliced
$^1/_2$ cucumber
50 g/2 oz radishes, sliced

FOR THE DRESSING
115 g/4 oz soft silken tofu
45 ml/3 tbsp milk
10 ml/2 tsp mustard
2.5 ml/$^1/_2$ tsp white wine vinegar
pinch of cayenne
salt and freshly ground black pepper

tofu *spring onions* *spinach leaves*

cherry tomatoes

avocado

white wine vinegar
mustard

cayenne *lime*

cucumber

radishes

milk

1 Cut the avocado in half, remove the stone and strip off the skin. Cut the flesh into slices. Transfer to a plate, drizzle over the lime juice and set aside.

2 Wash and dry the spinach leaves. Put them in a mixing bowl.

COOK'S TIP
Use soft silken tofu rather than the firm block variety. It can be found in most supermarkets in long-life cartons.

3 Cut the larger cherry tomatoes in half and add all the tomatoes to the mixing bowl, with the spring onions. Cut the cucumber into chunks and add to the bowl with the sliced radishes.

4 Make the dressing. Put the tofu, milk, mustard, wine vinegar and cayenne in a food processor or blender. Add salt and pepper to taste. Process for 30 seconds until smooth. Scrape the dressing into a bowl and add a little extra milk if you like a thinner dressing. Sprinkle with a little extra cayenne and garnish with radish roses and herb sprigs, if liked.

Asparagus Rolls with Herb Butter Sauce

For a taste sensation, try tender asparagus spears wrapped in crisp filo pastry. The buttery herb sauce makes the perfect accompaniment.

Serves 2

INGREDIENTS
4 sheets of filo pastry
50 g/2 oz/¼ cup butter, melted
16 young asparagus spears, trimmed

FOR THE SAUCE
2 shallots, finely chopped
1 bay leaf
150 ml/¼ pint/⅔ cup dry white wine
175 g/6 oz butter, softened
15 ml/1 tbsp chopped fresh herbs
salt and freshly ground black pepper
snipped chives, to garnish

fresh herbs

chives

dry white wine

asparagus spears

filo pastry   *butter*

bay leaf   *shallots*

1 Preheat the oven to 200°C/400°F/Gas 6. Brush each filo sheet with melted butter. Fold one corner of the sheet down to the bottom edge to give a wedge shape.

2 Lay 4 asparagus spears on top at the longest edge and roll up towards the shortest edge. Using the remaining filo and asparagus spears make 3 more rolls in the same way.

3 Lay the rolls on a greased baking sheet. Brush with the remaining melted butter. Bake in the oven for 8 minutes until golden.

4 Meanwhile, put the shallots, bay leaf and wine into a pan. Cover and cook over a high heat until the wine is reduced to about 45–60 ml/3–4 tbsp.

5 Strain the wine mixture into a bowl. Whisk in the butter, a little at a time, until the sauce is smooth and glossy.

6 Stir in the herbs and add salt and pepper to taste. Return to the pan and keep the sauce warm. Serve the rolls on individual plates with a salad garnish, if liked. Serve the butter sauce separately, sprinkled with a few snipped chives.

Tomato Omelette Envelopes

Delicious chive omelettes, folded and filled with tomato and melting Camembert cheese.

Serves 2

INGREDIENTS
1 small onion
4 tomatoes
30 ml/2 tbsp vegetable oil
4 eggs
30 ml/2 tbsp snipped fresh chives
115 g/4 oz Camembert cheese,
  rinded and diced
salt and freshly ground black pepper

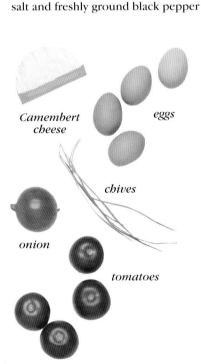

Camembert cheese

eggs

chives

onion

tomatoes

1 Cut the onion in half. Cut each half into thin wedges. Cut the tomatoes into wedges of similar size.

2 Heat 15 ml/1 tbsp of the oil in a frying pan. Cook the onion for 2 minutes over a moderate heat, then raise the heat and add the tomatoes. Cook for a further 2 minutes, then remove the pan from the heat.

3 Beat the eggs with the chives in a bowl. Add salt and pepper to taste. Heat the remaining oil in an omelette pan. Add half the egg mixture and tilt the pan to spread thinly. Cook for 1 minute.

4 Flip the omelette over and cook for 1 minute more. Remove from the pan and keep hot. Make a second omelette with the remaining egg mixture.

5 Return the tomato mixture to a high heat. Add the cheese and toss the mixture over the heat for 1 minute.

6 Divide the mixture between the omelettes and fold them over. Serve at once. Add crisp lettuce leaves and chunks of Granary bread, if liked.

COOK'S TIP
You may need to wipe the pan clean between the omelettes and reheat a little more oil.

Mushrooms with Leeks and Stilton

Upturned mushrooms make perfect containers for this leek and Stilton filling.

Serves 2–3

INGREDIENTS
1 leek, thinly sliced
6 flat mushrooms
2 garlic cloves, crushed
30 ml/2 tbsp chopped fresh parsley
115 g/4 oz/½ cup butter, softened
115 g/4 oz Stilton cheese
freshly ground black pepper
frisée and tomato halves, to garnish

leek

butter

flat mushrooms

parsley

Stilton cheese

garlic cloves

1 Put the leek slices in a small pan with a little water. Cover and cook for about 5 minutes until tender. Drain, refresh under cold water and drain again.

2 Remove the stalks from the mushrooms and set them aside. Put the mushroom caps, hollows uppermost, on an oiled baking sheet.

3 Put the mushroom stalks, garlic and parsley in a food processor or blender. Process for 1 minute. Tip into a bowl, add the leek and butter and season with freshly ground black pepper to taste. Preheat the grill.

4 Crumble the Stilton into the mushroom mixture and mix well. Divide the Stilton mixture between the mushroom caps and grill for 6–7 minutes until bubbling. Serve garnished with frisée and halved tomatoes.

Tomato and Okra Stew

Okra is an unusual and delicious vegetable. It releases a sticky sap when cooked, which helps to thicken the stew.

Serves 4

INGREDIENTS
15 ml/1 tbsp olive oil
1 onion, chopped
400 g/14 oz can pimientos, drained
2 x 400 g/14 oz cans chopped
 tomatoes
275 g/10 oz okra
30 ml/2 tbsp chopped fresh parsley
salt and freshly ground black pepper

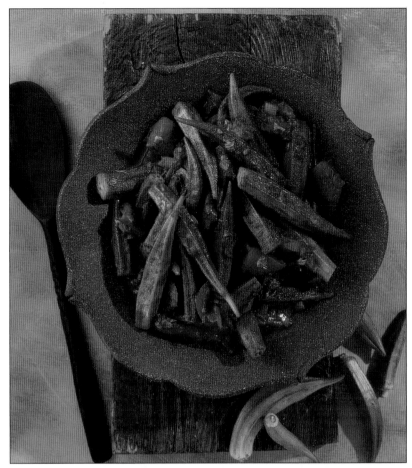

parsley

*chopped
tomatoes*

pimientos

onion

okra

1 Heat the oil in a pan. Add the onion and cook for 2–3 minutes.

2 Roughly chop the pimientos and add to the onion. Add the chopped tomatoes and mix well.

3 Cut the tops off the okra and cut into halves or quarters if large. Add to the tomato sauce in the pan. Season with plenty of salt and pepper.

4 Bring the vegetable stew to the boil, then lower the heat, cover the pan and simmer for 12 minutes until the vegetables are tender and the sauce has thickened. Stir in the chopped parsley and serve at once.

Vegetable Kebabs with Mustard and Honey

A colourful mixture of vegetables and tofu, skewered, glazed and grilled until tender.

Serves 4

INGREDIENTS
1 yellow pepper
2 small courgettes
225 g/8 oz piece of firm tofu
8 cherry tomatoes
8 button mushrooms
15 ml/1 tbsp wholegrain mustard
15 ml/1 tbsp clear honey
30 ml/2 tbsp olive oil
salt and freshly ground black pepper

TO SERVE
4 portions cooked mixed rice
  and wild rice
lime segments
flat leaf parsley

1 Cut the pepper in half and remove the seeds. Cut each half into quarters and cut each quarter in half.

2 Top and tail the courgettes and peel them decoratively, if you like. Cut each courgette into 8 chunks.

3 Cut the tofu into pieces of a similar size to the vegetables.

courgettes

cherry tomatoes

yellow pepper

clear honey

wholegrain mustard

button mushrooms

tofu

5 Whisk the mustard, honey and olive oil in a small bowl. Add salt and pepper to taste.

4 Thread the pepper pieces, courgette chunks, tofu, cherry tomatoes and mushrooms alternately on to four metal or bamboo skewers. Preheat the grill.

6 Put the kebabs on to a baking sheet. Brush with the mustard and honey glaze. Cook under the grill for 8 minutes, turning once or twice during cooking. Serve with a mixture of long grain and wild rice, and garnish with lime segments and parsley.

COOK'S TIP
If using bamboo skewers, soak them in a bowl of cold water before threading, to prevent them burning when placed under the grill.

Deep-fried Florets with Tangy Thyme Mayonnaise

Cauliflower and broccoli make a sensational snack when coated in a beer batter and deep-fried. Serve with a tangy mayonnaise.

Serves 2–3

INGREDIENTS
175 g/6 oz cauliflower
175 g/6 oz broccoli
2 eggs, separated
30 ml/2 tbsp olive oil
250 ml/8 fl oz/1 cup beer
150 ml/5 oz/1¼ cups plain flour
pinch of salt
30 ml/2 tbsp shredded fresh basil
vegetable oil for deep-frying
150 ml/¼ pint/⅔ cup good quality
  mayonnaise
10 ml/2 tsp chopped fresh thyme
10 ml/2 tsp grated lemon rind
10 ml/2 tsp lemon juice
sea salt, for sprinkling

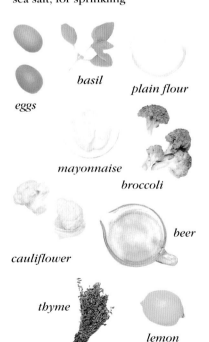

eggs

basil

plain flour

mayonnaise

broccoli

cauliflower

beer

thyme

lemon

1 Break the cauliflower and broccoli into small florets, cutting large florets into smaller pieces. Set aside.

2 Beat the egg yolks, olive oil, beer, flour and salt in a bowl. Strain the batter if necessary, to remove any lumps.

3 Whisk the egg whites until stiff. Fold into the batter with the basil.

4 Heat the oil for deep-frying to 180°C/350°F or until a cube of bread, when added to the oil, browns in 30–45 seconds. Dip the florets in the batter and deep-fry in batches for 2–3 minutes until the coating is golden and crisp. Drain on kitchen paper.

5 Mix the mayonnaise, thyme, lemon rind and juice in a small bowl.

6 Sprinkle the florets with sea salt. Serve with the thyme and lemon mayonnaise.

Black Bean and Vegetable Stir-fry

The secret of a quick stir-fry is to prepare all the ingredients first. This colourful vegetable mixture is coated in a classic Chinese sauce.

Serves 4

INGREDIENTS
8 spring onions
225 g/8 oz/2 cups button
 mushrooms
1 red pepper
1 green pepper
2 large carrots
60 ml/4 tbsp sesame oil
2 garlic cloves, crushed
60 ml/4 tbsp black bean sauce
90 ml/6 tbsp warm water
225 g/8 oz beansprouts
salt and freshly ground black pepper

1 Thinly slice the spring onions and button mushrooms.

2 Cut both the peppers in half, remove the seeds and slice the flesh into thin strips.

spring onions

black bean sauce

sesame oil

button mushrooms

red pepper

beansprouts

carrots

onion

garlic cloves

green pepper

3 Cut the carrots in half. Cut each half into thin strips lengthways. Stack the slices and cut through them to make very fine strips.

4 Heat the oil in a large wok or frying pan until very hot. Add the spring onions and garlic and stir-fry for 30 seconds.

5 Add the mushrooms, peppers and carrots. Stir-fry for 5–6 minutes over a high heat until the vegetables are just beginning to soften.

6 Mix the black bean sauce with the water. Add to the wok or pan and cook for 3–4 minutes. Stir in the beansprouts and stir-fry for 1 minute more, until all the vegetables are coated in the sauce. Season to taste. Serve at once.

COOK'S TIP
For best results the oil in the wok must be very hot before adding the vegetables.

French Bread Pizzas with Artichokes

Crunchy French bread makes an ideal base for these quick pizzas.

Serves 4

INGREDIENTS
15 ml/1 tbsp sunflower oil
1 onion, chopped
1 green pepper, seeded and
  chopped
200 g/7 oz can chopped tomatoes
15 ml/1 tbsp tomato purée
$1/2$ French stick
400 g/14 oz can artichoke
  hearts, drained
115 g/4 oz mozzarella cheese, sliced
15 ml/1 tbsp poppy seeds
salt and freshly ground black pepper

mozzarella cheese

French stick

tomato purée

chopped tomatoes

green pepper

poppy seeds

onion

artichoke hearts

1 Heat the oil in a frying pan. Add the chopped onion and pepper and cook for 4 minutes until just softened.

2 Stir in the chopped tomatoes and tomato purée. Cook for 4 minutes. Remove from the heat and add salt and pepper to taste.

3 Cut the piece of French stick in half lengthways. Cut each half in four to give eight pieces in all.

4 Spoon a little of the pepper and tomato mixture over each piece of bread. Preheat the grill.

5 Slice the artichoke hearts. Arrange them on top of the pepper and tomato mixture. Cover with the mozzarella slices and sprinkle with the poppy seeds.

6 Arrange the French bread pizzas on a rack over a grill pan and grill for 6–8 minutes until the cheese melts and is beginning to brown. Serve at once.

New Spring Salad

This chunky salad makes a satisfying meal, use other spring vegetables, if you like.

Serves 4

INGREDIENTS

675 g/1½ lb small new
  potatoes, halved
400 g/14 oz can broad
  beans, drained
115 g/4 oz cherry tomatoes
50 g/2 oz/2½ cups walnut halves
30 ml/2 tbsp white wine vinegar
15 ml/1 tbsp wholegrain mustard
60 ml/4 tbsp olive oil
pinch of sugar
225 g/8 oz young asparagus
  spears, trimmed
6 spring onions, trimmed
salt and freshly ground black pepper
baby spinach leaves, to serve

asparagus spears

new potatoes

wholegrain mustard

broad beans

cherry tomatoes

spring onions

walnut halves

1 Put the potatoes in a pan. Cover with cold water and bring to the boil. Cook for 10–12 minutes, until tender. Meanwhile, tip the broad beans into a bowl. Cut the tomatoes in half and add them to the bowl with the walnuts.

2 Put the white wine vinegar, mustard, olive oil and sugar into a jar. Add salt and pepper to taste. Close the jar tightly and shake well.

3 Add the asparagus to the potatoes and cook for 3 minutes more. Drain the cooked vegetables well, cool under cold running water and drain again. Thickly slice the potatoes. Cut the spring onions into halves.

4 Add the asparagus, potatoes and spring onions to the bowl containing the broad bean mixture. Pour the dressing over the salad and toss well. Serve on a bed of baby spinach leaves.

Brioche with Mixed Mushrooms

Mushrooms in a rich sherry sauce, served on toasted brioche, make a delectable lunch, but would also serve 6 as a starter.

Serves 4

INGREDIENTS

75 g/3 oz/6 tbsp butter
1 vegetable stock cube
450 g/1 lb shiitake mushrooms, caps only, sliced
225 g/8 oz button mushrooms, sliced
45 ml/3 tbsp dry sherry
250 ml/8 fl oz/1 cup crème fraîche
10 ml/2 tsp lemon juice
8 thick slices of brioche
salt and freshly ground black pepper

shiitake and button mushrooms   *brioche*

butter

stock cube   *crème fraîche*

lemon

COOK'S TIP

If shiitake mushrooms are too expensive or not available, substitute more button or brown cap mushrooms. Wipe the mushrooms with kitchen paper before use.

1 Melt the butter in a large pan. Crumble in the stock cube and stir for about 30 seconds.

2 Add the shiitake and button mushrooms to the pan and cook for 5 minutes over a moderate to high heat, stirring occasionally.

3 Stir in the sherry. Cook for 1 minute, then add the crème fraîche. Cook, stirring, over a gentle heat for 5 minutes. Stir in the lemon juice and add salt and pepper to taste. Preheat the grill.

4 Toast the brioche slices under the grill until just golden on both sides. Spoon the mushrooms on top, flash briefly under the grill, and serve. Fresh thyme may be used to garnish, if liked.

Ratatouille with Soft Cheese Croûtons

Crisp croûtons and creamy Camembert provide a tasty topping on hot ratatouille. Choose a quality brand of ratatouille or make your own.

Serves 2

INGREDIENTS
3 thick slices of white bread
225 g/8 oz firm Camembert cheese
60 ml/4 tbsp olive oil
1 garlic clove, chopped
400 g/14 oz can ratatouille
parsley sprigs, to garnish

ratatouille

parsley

garlic clove

Camembert cheese

white bread

1 Trim the crusts from the bread slices and discard. Cut the bread into 2.5 cm/1 in squares. Cut the Camembert into 2.5 cm/1 in cubes.

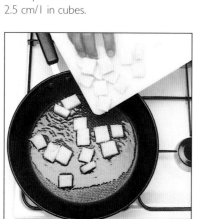

2 Heat 45 ml/3 tbsp of the oil in a frying pan. Add the bread and cook over a high heat for 5 minutes, stirring constantly, until golden all over. Reduce the heat, add the garlic and cook for 1 minute more. Remove the croûtons with a slotted spoon.

3 Tip the ratatouille into a pan and place over a medium heat, stirring occasionally, until hot.

4 Heat the remaining oil in the frying pan. Add the cheese cubes and sear over a high heat for 1 minute. Divide the hot ratatouille between two serving bowls, spoon the croûtons and cheese on top, garnish with the parsley and serve at once.

Ciabatta Rolls with Courgettes and Saffron

Split crunchy ciabatta rolls are filled with courgettes in a creamy tomato sauce flavoured with saffron. Use a mixture of green and yellow courgettes if possible.

Serves 4

INGREDIENTS
675 g/1½ lb small courgettes
15 ml/1 tbsp olive oil
2 shallots, freshly chopped
4 ciabatta rolls
200 g/7 oz can chopped tomatoes
pinch of sugar
a few saffron threads
50 ml/2 fl oz/¼ cup single cream
salt and freshly ground black pepper

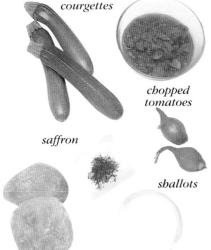

courgettes

chopped tomatoes

saffron

shallots

ciabatta rolls   single cream

COOK'S TIP

To avoid heating your oven, heat the rolls in a microwave. Put them on a plate, cover with kitchen paper and heat on HIGH for 30–45 seconds.

1 Preheat the oven to 180°C/350°F/ Gas 4. Top and tail the courgettes. Then, using a sharp knife, cut them into 4 cm/1½ in lengths, then cut each piece into quarters lengthways.

2 Heat the oil in a large frying pan. Add the shallots and fry over a moderate heat for 1–2 minutes. Put the rolls into the oven to warm through.

3 Add the courgettes to the shallots, mix well and cook for 6 minutes, stirring frequently, until just beginning to soften.

4 Stir in the tomatoes and sugar. Steep the saffron threads in a little hot water for a few minutes, then add to the pan with the cream. Cook for 4 minutes, stirring occasionally. Season to taste. Split open the rolls and fill with the courgettes and sauce.

Cheese en Croûte with Tomato Sauce

Melt-in-the-mouth cheese sandwiches, pan-fried and served with a tomato sauce.

Serves 4

INGREDIENTS
50 g/2 oz/¼ cup butter, softened
1 small onion, chopped
400 g/14 oz can chopped tomatoes
large thyme sprig
8 slices of white bread
115 g/4 oz mature Cheddar cheese
2 eggs
30 ml/2 tbsp milk
30 ml/2 tbsp groundnut oil
salt and freshly ground black pepper
8 cos lettuce leaves, to serve

thyme

eggs

chopped tomatoes

onion

milk

Cheddar cheese

butter

white bread

1 Melt 25 g/1 oz/2 tbsp of the butter in a frying pan. Add the onion and cook for 3–4 minutes until soft.

2 Stir in the chopped tomatoes. Strip the leaves from the thyme sprig and stir them into the pan. Add salt and pepper to taste, then cover the pan and cook for 5 minutes.

3 Meanwhile, spread the remaining butter over the slices of bread.

4 Slice the cheese thinly. Arrange on 4 slices of bread and sandwich with the remaining slices. Trim the crusts.

5 Beat the eggs and milk together in a bowl. Add salt and pepper to taste and pour into a shallow dish.

6 Heat the oil in a large frying pan. Dip each sandwich in the egg mixture until well-coated. Add to the hot oil and fry for 2 minutes on each side, until the coating is golden and the cheese has melted. Cut each sandwich into quarters. Arrange on individual plates garnished with the cos lettuce leaves. Serve the tomato sauce in a bowl to one side.

COOK'S TIP
If the tomato sauce is a little tart, add a pinch of sugar, or liven it up with a dash of Tabasco.

Potato, Broccoli and Red Pepper Stir-fry

A hot and hearty stir-fry of vegetables with just a hint of fresh ginger.

Serves 2

INGREDIENTS

450 g/1 lb potatoes
45 ml/3 tbsp groundnut oil
50 g/2 oz/¼ cup butter
1 small onion, chopped
1 red pepper, seeded and chopped
225 g/8 oz broccoli, broken
  into florets
2.5 cm/1 in piece of fresh root
  ginger, peeled and grated
salt and freshly ground black pepper

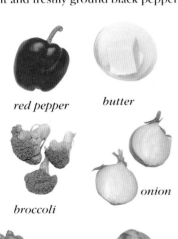

red pepper   *butter*

broccoli   *onion*

root ginger   *potatoes*

COOK'S TIP

Although a wok is the preferred pan for stir-frying, for this recipe a flat frying pan is best to cook the potatoes quickly.

1 Peel the potatoes and cut them into 1 cm/½ in dice.

2 Heat the oil in a large frying pan and add the potatoes. Cook for 8 minutes over a high heat, stirring and tossing occasionally, until the potatoes are browned and just tender.

3 Drain off the oil. Add the butter to the potatoes in the pan. As soon as it melts, add the onion and red pepper. Stir-fry for 2 minutes.

4 Add the broccoli florets and ginger to the pan. Stir-fry for 2–3 minutes more, taking care not to break up the potatoes. Add salt and pepper to taste and serve at once.

Bubble and Squeak with Fried Eggs

Next time you are serving mashed potato, make double the amount and chill half so that you can make this tasty dish the next day.

Serves 2

INGREDIENTS
½ Savoy cabbage
50 g/2 oz/¼ cup butter
1 small onion, finely chopped
450 g/1 lb mashed potato
15 ml/1 tbsp chopped fresh parsley
15 ml/1 tbsp vegetable oil
2 eggs
salt and freshly ground black pepper
2 tomatoes, halved, to serve

eggs

mashed potato

butter

onion

Savoy cabbage

parsley

1 Cut out and discard the hard core of the cabbage. Strip off and discard the outer layer of leaves. Finely slice the remaining cabbage and set aside.

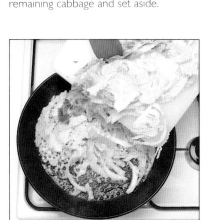

2 Melt the butter in a large frying pan. Add the onion and fry for 2–3 minutes until just tender. Reduce the heat slightly, add the cabbage and cook, stirring constantly, for 2–3 minutes.

3 Add the mashed potato to the pan. Stir to combine. Cook for 5–6 minutes until the mixture starts to brown. Stir in the chopped parsley and add salt and pepper to taste. Transfer the mixture to a serving dish and keep hot.

4 Wipe the pan clean. Heat the oil and fry the eggs until just set. Serve the bubble and squeak on individual plates, adding a fried egg and two tomato halves to each portion. Sprinkle with black pepper.

Potato, Spinach and Pine Nut Gratin

Pine nuts add a satisfying crunch to this gratin of wafer-thin potato slices and spinach in a creamy cheese sauce.

Serves 2

INGREDIENTS
450 g/1 lb potatoes
1 garlic clove, crushed
3 spring onions, thinly sliced
150 ml/¹/₄ pint/²/₃ cup single cream
250 ml/8 fl oz/1 cup milk
225 g/8 oz frozen chopped
  spinach, thawed
115 g/4 oz Cheddar cheese, grated
25 g/1 oz/¹/₄ cup pine nuts
salt and freshly ground black pepper

spinach *potatoes*

garlic clove

pine nuts

spring onions

Cheddar cheese

single cream

1 Peel the potoates and cut them carefully into wafer-thin slices. Spread them out in a large, heavy-based, non-stick frying pan.

2 Scatter the crushed garlic and sliced spring onions evenly over the potatoes.

3 Pour the cream and milk over the potatoes. Place the pan over a gentle heat, cover and cook for 8 minutes or until the potatoes are tender.

4 Using both hands, squeeze the spinach dry. Add the spinach to the potatoes, mixing lightly. Cover the pan and cook for 2 minutes more.

5 Add salt and pepper to taste, then spoon the mixture into a gratin dish. Preheat the grill.

6 Sprinkle the grated cheese and pine nuts over the spinach mixture. Heat under the grill for 2–3 minutes until the topping is golden. A simple lettuce and tomato salad makes an excellent accompaniment to this dish.

Creamy Cannellini Beans with Asparagus

Cannellini beans in a creamy sauce contrast with tender asparagus in this tasty toast topper.

Serves 2

INGREDIENTS
10 ml/2 tsp butter
1 small onion, finely chopped
1 small carrot, grated
5 ml/1 tsp fresh thyme leaves
400 g/14 oz can cannellini
  beans, drained
150 ml/¼ pint/⅔ cup single cream
115 g/4 oz young asparagus
  spears, trimmed
2 slices of fresh cut Granary bread
salt and freshly ground black pepper

Granary bread *carrot* *thyme*

butter

asparagus spears

single cream

onion

cannellini beans

parsley

1 Melt the butter in a pan. Add the onion and carrot and fry over a moderate heat for 4 minutes until soft. Add the thyme leaves.

2 Rinse the cannellini beans under cold running water. Drain thoroughly, then add to the onion and carrot. Mix lightly.

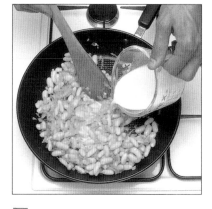

3 Pour in the cream and heat slowly to just below boiling point, stirring occasionally. Remove the pan from the heat and add salt and pepper to taste. Preheat the grill.

4 Place the asparagus spears in a saucepan. Pour over just enough boiling water to cover. Poach for 3–4 minutes until the spears are just tender.

5 Meanwhile, toast the bread under the grill until both sides are golden.

6 Place the toast on individual plates. Drain the asparagus and divide the spears between the slices of toast. Spoon the bean mixture over each portion and serve.

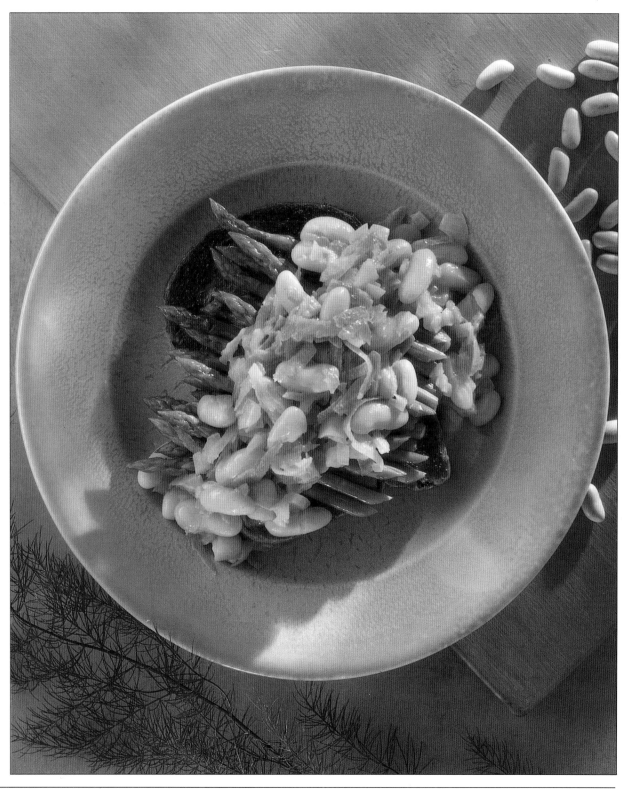

COOK'S TIP
Use your favourite variety of canned beans such as borlotti, haricot or flageolets.

Red Fried Rice

This vibrant rice dish owes its appeal as much to the bright colours of red onion, red pepper and cherry tomatoes as it does to their distinctive flavours.

Serves 2

INGREDIENTS
115 g/4 oz/³/₄ cup basmati rice
30 ml/2 tbsp groundnut oil
1 small red onion, chopped
1 red pepper, seeded and chopped
225 g/8 oz cherry tomatoes, halved
2 eggs, beaten
salt and freshly ground black pepper

eggs

basmati rice

cherry tomatoes

red onion

red pepper

1 Wash the rice several times under cold running water. Drain well. Bring a large pan of water to the boil, add the rice and cook for 10–12 minutes.

2 Meanwhile, heat the oil in a wok until very hot. Add the onion and red pepper and stir-fry for 2–3 minutes. Add the cherry tomatoes and stir-fry for a further 2 minutes.

3 Pour in the beaten eggs all at once. Cook for 30 seconds without stirring, then stir to break up the egg as it sets.

4 Drain the cooked rice thoroughly, add to the wok and toss it over the heat with the vegetable and egg mixture for 3 minutes. Season the fried rice with salt and pepper to taste.

Chick-pea Stew

This hearty chick-pea and vegetable stew makes a filling meal. It is delicious served with garlic-flavoured mashed potato.

Serves 4

INGREDIENTS

30 ml/2 tbsp olive oil
1 small onion, chopped
225 g/8 oz carrots, halved
  and thinly sliced
2.5 ml/½ tsp ground cumin
5 ml/1 tsp ground coriander
30 ml/2 tbsp plain flour
225 g/8 oz courgettes, sliced
200 g/7 oz can sweetcorn, drained
400 g/14 oz can chick-peas, drained
30 ml/2 tbsp tomato purée
200 ml/7 fl oz/scant 1 cup hot
  vegetable stock
salt and freshly ground black pepper

onion

tomato purée

sweetcorn

chick-peas

stock cube

ground cumin

plain flour

ground coriander

carrots

courgettes

1 Heat the oil in a frying pan. Add the onion and carrots. Toss to coat the vegetables in the oil, then cook over moderate heat for 4 minutes.

2 Add the ground cumin, coriander and flour. Stir and cook for 1 minute.

COOK'S TIP

For speedy garlic-flavoured mashed potatoes simply mash potatoes with garlic butter and stir in chopped fresh parsley and a little crème fraîche.

3 Cut the courgette slices in half. Add them to the pan with the sweetcorn, chick-peas, tomato purée and vegetable stock. Stir well. Cook for 10 minutes, stirring frequently.

4 Taste the stew and add salt and pepper. Serve at once, with garlic-flavoured mashed potato (see Cook's Tip), if liked.

Aubergine Pilaff

This hearty dish is made with bulgur wheat and aubergine, flavoured with fresh mint.

Serves 2

INGREDIENTS
2 medium aubergines
60-90 ml/4-6 tbsp sunflower oil
1 small onion, finely chopped
175 g/6 oz/1 cup bulgur wheat
450 ml/16 fl oz/scant 2 cups
  vegetable stock
30 ml/2 tbsp pine nuts, toasted
15 ml/1 tbsp chopped fresh mint
salt and freshly ground black pepper

FOR THE GARNISH
lime wedges
lemon wedges
torn mint leaves

COOK'S TIP
To cut down on the cooking time, soak the bulgur wheat in water to cover by 2.5 cm/1 in for up to 8 hours. Drain and continue as described in the recipe, reducing the cooking time to 8 minutes.

1 Trim the ends from the aubergines. Using a sharp knife, cut them into neat sticks and then into 1 cm/½ in dice.

2 Heat 60 ml/4 tbsp of the oil in a large frying pan. Add the onion and sauté for 1 minute.

3 Add the diced aubergine. Cook over a high heat, stirring frequently, for about 4 minutes until just tender. Add the remaining oil if needed.

4 Stir in the bulgur wheat, mixing well, then pour in the vegetable stock. Bring to the boil, then lower the heat and simmer for 10 minutes or until all the liquid has evaporated. Season to taste.

5 Add the pine nuts, stir gently with a wooden spoon, then stir in the mint.

6 Spoon the pilaff on to individual plates and garnish each portion with lime and lemon wedges. Sprinkle with torn mint leaves for extra colour.

Houmus with Pan-fried Courgettes

Pan-fried courgettes are perfect for dipping into home-made houmus.

Serves 4

INGREDIENTS
225 g/8 oz can chick-peas
2 garlic cloves, roughly chopped
90 ml/6 tbsp lemon juice
60 ml/4 tbsp tahini paste
75 ml/5 tbsp olive oil, plus extra
  to serve
5 ml/1 tsp ground cumin
450 g/1 lb small courgettes
salt and freshly ground black pepper

TO SERVE
paprika
pitta bread
black olives

courgettes

chick-peas   *lemon*

tahini paste

garlic cloves

ground cumin

1 Drain the chick-peas, reserving the liquid from the can, and tip them into a food processor or blender. Blend to a smooth purée, adding a small amount of the reserved liquid if necessary.

2 Mix the garlic, lemon juice and tahini together and add to the food processor or blender. Process until smooth. With the machine running, gradually add 45 ml/3 tbsp of the olive oil through the feeder tube or lid.

3 Add the cumin, with salt and pepper to taste. Process to mix, then scrape the houmus into a bowl. Cover and chill until required.

4 Top and tail the courgettes. Slice them lengthways into even-size pieces.

5 Heat the remaining oil in a large frying pan. Season the courgettes and fry them for 2–3 minutes on each side until just tender.

COOK'S TIP
Houmus is also delicious served with pan-fried or grilled aubergine slices.

6 Divide the courgettes among four individual plates. Spoon a portion of houmus on to each plate, sprinkle with paprika, add two or three pieces of sliced pitta bread and serve with olives.

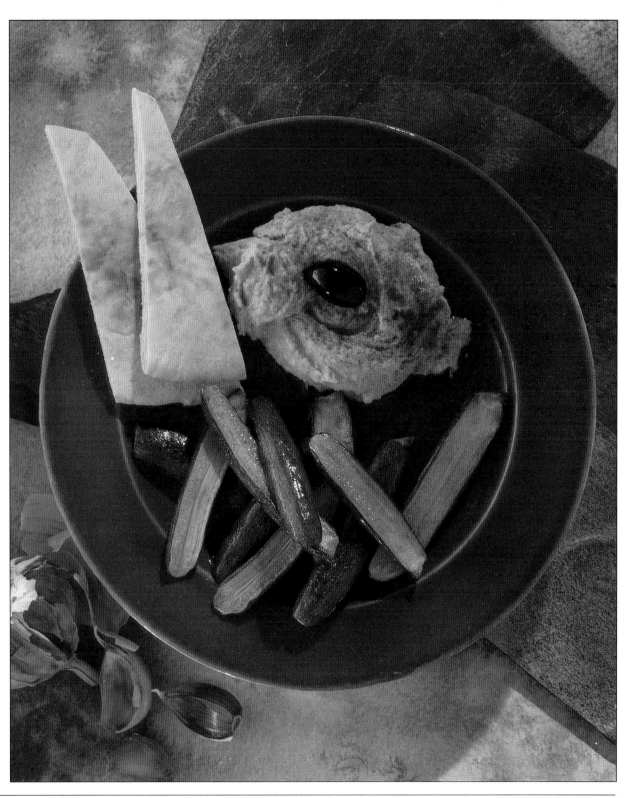

Lentil Stir-fry

Mushrooms, artichokes, sugar snap peas and lentils make a satisfying stir-fry supper.

Serves 2–3

INGREDIENTS

115 g/4 oz sugar snap peas
25 g/1 oz butter
1 small onion, chopped
115 g/4 oz cup or brown cap
  mushrooms, sliced
400 g/14 oz can artichoke hearts,
  drained and halved
400 g/14 oz can green
  lentils, drained
60 ml/4 tbsp single cream
25 g/1 oz/¼ cup flaked
  almonds, toasted
salt and freshly ground black pepper
French bread, to serve

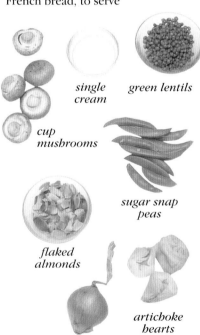

single cream *green lentils*

cup mushrooms

sugar snap peas

flaked almonds

artichoke hearts

onion

COOK'S TIP
Use Greek yogurt instead of the cream, if preferred.

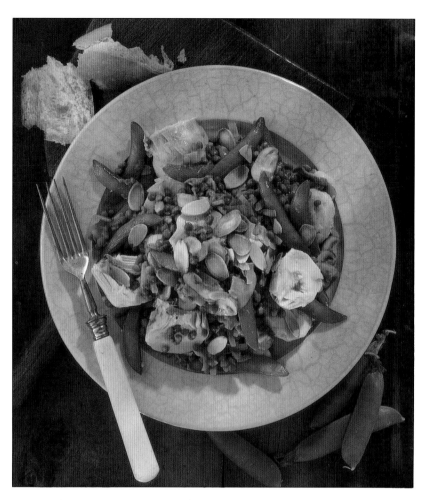

1 Bring a pan of salted water to the boil, add the sugar snap peas and cook for about 4 minutes until just tender. Drain, refresh under cold running water, then drain again. Pat dry the peas with kitchen paper and set aside.

2 Melt the butter in a frying pan. Cook the chopped onion for 2–3 minutes, stirring occasionally.

3 Add the sliced mushrooms to the onion. Stir until combined, then cook for 2–3 minutes until just tender. Add the artichokes, sugar snap peas and lentils to the pan. Stir-fry for 2 minutes.

4 Stir in the cream and almonds and cook for 1 minute. Season to taste. Serve at once, with chunks of French bread.

Nut Pilaff with Omelette Rolls

A wonderful mixture of textures – soft fluffy rice with crunchy nuts and omelette rolls.

Serves 2

INGREDIENTS
175 g/6 oz/1 cup basmati rice
15 ml/1 tbsp sunflower oil
1 small onion, chopped
1 red pepper, finely diced
350 ml/12 fl oz/1½ cups hot
  vegetable stock
2 eggs
25 g/1 oz/¼ cup salted peanuts
15 ml/1 tbsp soy sauce
salt and freshly ground black pepper
parsley sprigs, to garnish

salted peanuts

parsley

onion

eggs

stock cube

basmati rice

red pepper

soy sauce

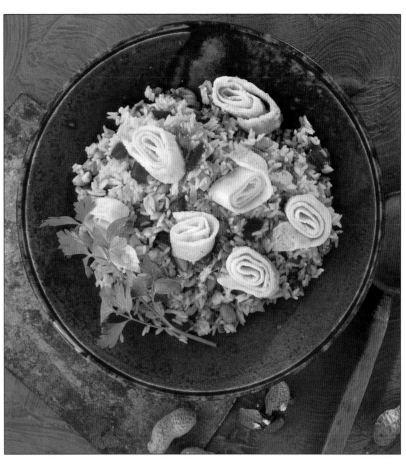

1 Wash the rice several times under cold running water. Drain thoroughly. Heat half the oil in a large frying pan. Fry the onion and pepper for 2–3 minutes then stir in the rice and stock. Bring to the boil and cook for 10 minutes until the rice is tender.

2 Meanwhile, beat the eggs lightly with salt and pepper to taste. Heat the remaining oil in a second large frying pan. Pour in the eggs and tilt the pan to cover the base thinly. Cook the omelette for 1 minute, then flip it over and cook the other side for 1 minute.

3 Slide the omelette on to a clean board and roll it up tightly. Cut the omelette roll into 8 slices.

4 Stir the peanuts and the soy sauce into the pilaff and add black pepper to taste. Turn the pilaff into a serving dish, arrange the omelette rolls on top and garnish with the parsley. Serve at once.

Kedgeree with French Beans and Mushrooms

Crunchy French beans and mushrooms are the star ingredients in this vegetarian version of an old favourite.

Serves 2

INGREDIENTS

115 g/4 oz/³/₄ cup basmati rice
3 eggs
175 g/6 oz French beans, trimmed
50 g/2 oz/¹/₄ cup butter
1 onion, finely chopped
225 g/8 oz brown cap mushrooms,
  quartered
30 ml/2 tbsp single cream
15 ml/1 tbsp chopped fresh parsley
salt and freshly ground black pepper

single cream

brown cap mushrooms

parsley

onion

butter

French beans

eggs

basmati rice

1 Wash the rice several times under cold running water. Drain thoroughly. Bring a pan of water to the boil, add the rice and cook for 10–12 minutes until tender. Drain thoroughly.

2 Half fill a second pan with water, add the eggs and bring to the boil. Lower the heat and simmer for 8 minutes. Drain the eggs, cool them under cold water, then remove the shells.

3 Bring another pan of water to the boil and cook the French beans for 5 minutes. Drain, refresh under cold running water, then drain again.

4 Melt the butter in a large frying pan. Add the onion and mushrooms. Cook for 2–3 minutes over a moderate heat.

5 Add the French beans and rice to the onion mixture. Stir lightly to mix. Cook for 2 minutes. Cut the hard-boiled eggs in wedges and add them to the pan.

6 Stir in the cream and parsley, taking care not to break up the eggs. Reheat the kedgeree, but do not allow it to boil. Serve at once.

Chick-pea Falafel with Coriander Dip

Little balls of spicy chick-pea purée, deep-fried until crisp, are served together with a coriander-flavoured mayonnaise.

Serves 4

INGREDIENTS
400 g/14 oz can chick-peas, drained
6 spring onions, finely sliced
1 egg
2.5 ml/½ tsp ground turmeric
1 garlic clove, crushed
5 ml/1 tsp ground cumin
60 ml/4 tbsp chopped
    fresh coriander
oil for deep-frying
1 small red chilli, seeded and
    finely chopped
45 ml/3 tbsp mayonnaise
salt and freshly ground black pepper
coriander sprig, to garnish

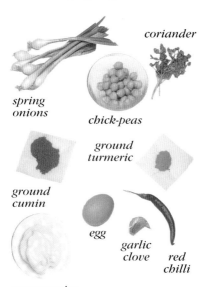

coriander

spring onions

chick-peas

ground turmeric

ground cumin

egg

garlic clove

red chilli

mayonnaise

COOK'S TIP
If you have time, chill the chick-pea purée before making it into balls. It will be easier to shape.

1 Tip the chick-peas into a food processor or blender. Add the spring onions and process to a smooth purée. Add the egg, turmeric, garlic, cumin and 15 ml/1 tbsp of the chopped coriander. Process briefly to mix, then add salt and pepper to taste.

2 Working with clean wet hands, shape the chick-pea mixture into about 16 small balls.

3 Heat the oil for deep-frying to 180°C/350°F or until a cube of bread, when added to the oil, browns in 30–45 seconds. Deep-fry the falafel in batches for 2–3 minutes or until golden. Drain on kitchen paper, then place in a serving bowl.

4 Stir the remaining coriander and the chilli into the mayonnaise. Garnish with the coriander sprig and serve alongside the falafel.

Three Bean Salad with Yogurt Dressing

This tangy bean and pasta salad is great on its own or can be served as a side dish.

Serves 3–4

INGREDIENTS
75 g/3 oz penne or other dried
  pasta shapes
2 tomatoes
200 g/7 oz can red kidney
  beans, drained
200 g/7 oz can cannellini
  beans, drained
200 g/7 oz can chick-peas, drained
1 green pepper, seeded and diced
75 ml/3 tbsp natural yogurt
30 ml/2 tbsp sunflower oil
grated rind of ¹/₂ lemon
10 ml/2 tsp wholegrain mustard
5 ml/1 tsp chopped fresh oregano
salt and freshly ground black pepper

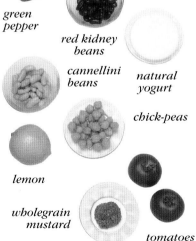

oregano *penne*

green pepper

red kidney beans

cannellini beans *natural yogurt*

chick-peas

lemon

wholegrain mustard

tomatoes

1 Bring a large pan of salted water to the boil. Add the pasta and cook for 10–12 minutes until just tender. Drain, cool under cold water and drain again.

2 Make a cross with the tip of a sharp knife in each of the tomatoes. Plunge them into a bowl of boiling water for 30 seconds. Remove with a slotted spoon or spatula, run under cold water and peel away the skins. Cut the tomatoes into segments.

3 Drain the canned beans and chick-peas in a colander, rinse them under cold water and drain again. Tip into a bowl. Add the tomato segments, green pepper and pasta.

4 Whisk the yogurt until smooth. Gradually whisk in the oil, lemon rind and mustard. Stir in the oregano and salt and pepper to taste. Pour the dressing over the salad and toss well.

INDEX